ARM YOURSELF

Equipping Ourselves with
the Armor of God

Michelle Moore

Sachse Public Library

Copyright © 2014 Michelle Moore.

All rights reserved. No part of this book may be used or reproduced by any means, graphic, electronic, or mechanical, including photocopying, recording, taping or by any information storage retrieval system without the written permission of the publisher except in the case of brief quotations embodied in critical articles and reviews.

Scriptures taken from the Holy Bible, New International Version®, NIV®. Copyright © 1973, 1978, 1984, 2011 by Biblica, Inc.™ Used by permission of Zondervan. All rights reserved worldwide. www.zondervan.com The "NIV" and "New International Version" are trademarks registered in the United States Patent and Trademark Office by Biblica, Inc.™ All rights reserved.

Scripture quotations taken from the Holy Bible, New Living Translation, copyright 1996, 2004. Used by permission of Tyndale House Publishers, Inc., Wheaton, Illinois 60189. All rights reserved. All Scripture quotations in this publications are from The Message. Copyright (c) by Eugene H. Peterson 1993, 1994, 1995, 1996, 2000, 2001, 2002. Used by permission of NavPress Publishing Group.

Scripture taken from the Amplified Bible, Copyright © 1954, 1958, 1962, 1964, 1965, 1987 by The Lockman Foundation. Used by permission.

WestBow Press books may be ordered through booksellers or by contacting:

WestBow Press
A Division of Thomas Nelson & Zondervan
1663 Liberty Drive
Bloomington, IN 47403
www.westbowpress.com
1 (866) 928-1240

Because of the dynamic nature of the Internet, any web addresses or links contained in this book may have changed since publication and may no longer be valid. The views expressed in this work are solely those of the author and do not necessarily reflect the views of the publisher, and the publisher hereby disclaims any responsibility for them.

Any people depicted in stock imagery provided by Thinkstock are models, and such images are being used for illustrative purposes only. Certain stock imagery © Thinkstock.

ISBN: 978-1-4908-4887-7 (sc)
ISBN: 978-1-4908-4888-4 (hc)
ISBN: 978-1-4908-4886-0 (e)

Library of Congress Control Number: 2014915090

Printed in the United States of America.

WestBow Press rev. date: 09/08/2014

Dedicated to

My husband, Lyndsey, who gave me his full support through this entire process and was my biggest cheerleader...

and my boys, Caleb and Brayden, that I hope to leave a legacy of faith for.

I also dedicate this book to my grandma and grandpa Castro who inspired me and encouraged me to always live for Jesus...

and to my mom, Sherrie, who always prayed the Armor of God over me.

"The night is nearly over; the day is almost here. So let us put aside the deeds of darkness and put on the armor of light."
Romans 13:12

Contents

1. My Battle 1

2. The Shield of Faith 19

3. The Belt of Truth 44

4. The Helmet of Salvation 56

5. The Shoes of Peace 69

6. The Breastplate of Righteousness 79

7. The Sword of the Spirit 87

8. The Robe of Love 99

9. The Power of Prayer 115

1

My Battle

"For our struggle is not against flesh and blood, but against the rulers, against the authorities, against the powers of this dark world and against the spiritual forces of evil in the heavenly realms"
Ephesians 6:12

I was standing in the middle of a valley. It was eerily quiet with the wind whipping around me. I felt scared, alone, and lost. I looked to my left and saw an army of death. The riders on the horses were covered in black armor and there were frightening creatures near the floor that looked a lot like demons. They were full of hatred and anger. They looked ravenous. I was terrified.

I looked to my right and saw an army of peace. There were riders in white, glowing with iridescence. The rider up front was the largest. He sat on a beautiful white horse covered in beautiful pearl-like armor and held his sword up high. All around him seemed to be angelic beings and everyone looked like they were ready for battle.

But why? What were they fighting for? Then at once both armies ran forward shouting their battle cries and I felt as though I was stuck in the middle of a battle scene from Lord of the Rings. As they came closer, I realized something. They were coming closer and closer and I was standing in the middle. Then a realization hit me... *they were fighting for me!* It was all I could do to keep myself from running away, but my feet were stuck. I threw myself down to the ground and covered my head with my arms just as the two armies were about to collide and then... I woke up.

Awake

I was only nine years old when I had that dream. It was my first glimpse into the spiritual realm and the battle being fought over my life. I woke up with a sense of urgency and knew that a line was being drawn and I needed to choose which side, which army.

I had already been dealing with terrible bouts of anxiety, depression and episodes of harmful thoughts. These terrible things were brought forth from some unfortunate events that happened to me just a couple of years prior. Unfortunately, I was plagued with guilt and shame which fed the lie that it was all my fault. I had a difficult time learning to deal with such heavy emotions, thoughts, and feelings that consumed me day in and day out.

When I awoke from that dream I knew exactly whose side I would choose. I knew who I wanted behind me, and I accepted the Lord as my savior at nine years old. I was baptized later that year on the Fourth of July. It was a day that will forever stay with me as I not only celebrate my freedom in this country but my freedom in Christ. I am grateful that at such a young age God called me, beckoned me, and I had the mind about me to answer His call with a resounding yes!

But my testimony doesn't stop there...no, my battle had only just begun. I continued to struggle with some of those issues. But after fervent prayers from a little girl with a renewed sense of hope and a mother that knew how to intercede, I was freed from that debilitating condition and not long after, I got my childhood back.

So I continued to grow and act relatively normal. I always had in the back of my mind that I wanted to forget that part of my life. I prayed, as I got older, that the Lord would erase parts of my brain that had anything to do with that period of time. I didn't want to remember it, didn't want anything to do with it, and wanted to go on with my life as I planned. So in my teenage years, that is exactly what I did. I had the attitude that this was my life and I will live it how I see fit. But when you give a teenage girl a car and freedom, you might run into a problem or two.

You see, although my mom was a great source of strength and a positive influence for me when I was younger, she also had her own set of issues to work through. My mother suffered from some serious health issues after going through a total hysterectomy at an early age. It threw her into a tailspin of hormones and more and more sickness. She withered down to about 98 pounds.

My parent's marriage also began to crumble and there were days she didn't even want to get out of bed, not even to drive me to school. This began to show serious consequences when I got a truancy letter from the high school, warning me that if I received anymore unexcused absences, they would be seeing us in court.

During this time we also would go down to the altar almost every single Sunday at church and ask for healing in my mom. She would be praying and fall out in the spirit and the next day, she would be...the same. I didn't understand it and I was frustrated with God. *Why did my mom have to keep suffering? Where was her healing? Why did I have to grow up so fast? Why couldn't my mom take care of me like she used to? Where did her strength go? Why do my parents argue all the time?* I couldn't understand the heartache and the hurt. So with my determination to forget my past, I no longer remembered what God was capable of. I forgot the dream I had when I was younger and I began to forge one out for myself.

Well by my junior year of high school, my mother had recovered. She got a part time job at Family Christian store and a renewed sense of hope and of mothering. I, on the other hand, had a car and an attitude. I thought, *How dare she think she can just walk right back into being my mom again? I can take care of myself!* So needless to say, we did not get a long very well. I would abide by her curfew boundaries and do what I was told at home, so then I could leave the house and do what I wanted.

I got into a relationship with a boy during that time that was very unhealthy. I became someone I knew deep down I was not. I hated myself for it. I knew I was living a lie and I was not in the right place in my heart, mind, or soul. The way my rebellion came out was bitterness toward my mom, and I would spew anger at her.

I was losing myself in my boyfriend, my friends, my music and I became sick, literally. Anytime I was about to go out and do something I knew I shouldn't, I would literally vomit before I left the house. I went anyways, despite the conviction I felt deep within my heart.

Please understand this though, I had accepted Christ as my Savior and I believe that with that comes the power of God's sweet Holy Spirit. He never left me even when I was in sin and full of hurt and pain and questioning my faith. He was there, whispering me to stop what I was doing and I knew it, felt it, but what did I do? Everything I could to suppress it! I lost my innocence and had my first taste of alcohol at 16 years old at a college party.

My mom had shortly before that given me a brand new bible for my birthday with the instructions to "read it because I needed it". I praise God that I did! I praise God that I was never too stubborn, never too hard hearted to know when it was time to stop and listen.

One day when my boyfriend had a date planned for me and I knew I would be spending all day with him, I could not get out of bed. My stomach was twisted in knots from the stress, and I couldn't keep anything down. So while laying in my bed with a heavy heart, I called out to God, *What is wrong with me? What is this? Why do I feel so sick?* I heard the Lord tell me, *"This is not what I have planned for you. I have been trying to tell you, but you won't listen. I have to literally stop you in your tracks so that you could hear me. I have such greater things planned for you."*

I got out of bed and knew exactly what I needed to do. I drove over to my boyfriend's house and knocked on his door, broke up with him, walked out of his house and never saw him again. I felt terrible! I felt guilty for breaking his heart with not much more than an explanation of "We are not meant to be and I am not suppose to be with you." I left him at his door with his mouth open and he was very upset. He called and called and I knew that I was supposed to cut all ties and move on. I knew that when God told me to do something, I was going to do it, all or nothing. I changed my number and refused any contact from him, email or otherwise. Sounds harsh, but my stomach stopped being sick.

I was dealt another blow. Satan fed me lies of guilt and shame after that incident. I kept replaying his tears and broken heart over and over in mind till I fell right back down into the mess

I thought I had forgotten. I couldn't sleep, couldn't be happy. I couldn't eat, didn't feel I deserved to. I thought, *I just broke someone's heart and cut him off! How do I expect to just go on carefree and happy?*

I began to open up my Bible and seek wisdom from the Lord. I would ask Him, *Ok Lord, I did what you told me, now what? I am torn up inside from hurt, shame and guilt. I am lost and need to fight this once again. Help me overcome this. You did it before and I know you can help me overcome this again!* My mom stepped in like the mom I always knew she was, and since she worked at a Christian bookstore I had ample resources at my disposal.

I began reading books by Beth Moore and many other famous Christian authors. One of hers that I clung to during that time was *Praying God's Word*. I believe there is immense power over praying Scripture over your life and your situation, which we will later go into. It was as if the metal chains holding me down were melting off of me.

Then I received *Battlefield of the Mind* by Joyce Meyer. It truly changed my life and my thinking, and I was never the same. This difficult time didn't last nearly as long as the last and instead of asking God to make me forget, I asked Him, *Lord, help me to remember your mercy and grace.*

My First Armor Experience

I remember my mom would pray the Armor of God over me every morning, on the way to school. She would touch my head when mentioning the helmet, my hands when mentioning the shield and sword, and so on. I remember thinking it was a little strange, but I let my mom pray over me and I went about my day. Little did I know the power it would harness later in my life. I did not quite fully understand it, but God honored my mother's prayer.

I believe I was shown a lot at a young age, grew up faster and was equipped with the weapons of warfare to face what Satan wanted to destroy. He wants to tear apart a young girl full of fresh faith. I am thankful I was protected from a lot of his attacks because of my mother's prayers.

I was young, but I was learning these lessons, growing and slowly evolving into the person I was created for. I gave him my all, my future husband, future dreams, and future children. One of the revelations God gave me during this time was that the devil was trying to place mental strongholds on me and use his old schemes and tricks to see if they could swallow me up like before.

You see, although I began to grow seed in my life, it would be quickly washed away because my roots were not very deep yet, as in the Parable of the Sower. So I asked God to remove me from anything in my life that wasn't suppose to be there. I lost some friends and made some new ones.

The incredible thing was that at the same time God was working on me, he was also working on my future husband. God redeemed and restored him from a past that had been fueled with drugs, alcohol, and women. He was a good friend of the family and we grew up in church together. After a long friendship and allowing the Lord to bring healing, God penned our love story and I got the privilege to marry my best friend. Had I not listened to the Holy Spirit's nudging, had I ignored Him leading me to a better future than I could have ever imagined, I would have had a much different outcome.

We led bible studies out of our homes when we were engaged, talked about the Lord together, and saved ourselves for marriage knowing God would honor that decision and restore our purity through his awesome mercy. I was thankful for the close relationship I shared with the Lord and the incredible marriage I looked forward to.

Life's Realities

Well fast forward 10 years and it looks something like this: we went through three apartments, two years of living with family, two houses, left our home church, both of us returned to college, several health scares, two kids, financial difficulties resulting in burdensome debt, all while sprinkling a lot of family drama or shall I say chaos along the way. I was close to God but man did all of my circumstances seem to drown that out really quickly.

I believe that when you have already learned your lesson by going through something once, don't make the same mistake again, you can really save yourself a lot of heartache. I had to learn that lesson the hard way through many different areas of my life. I began to get complacent and comfortable. Ignoring any conviction in my spirit was an old habit that hadn't quite died hard or even at all. I allowed a lot of things back into my life that I thought I had put down for good. You know the old saying, "Garbage in, garbage out"? Well let's just say I began slowly letting a lot of garbage in that had no business being there.

My husband was out of town on business a lot through our marriage. I never liked it when he left, and when our kids were babies I would always ask for help and complain about him not being there. I began to depend on him, perhaps too much. When I felt he could not make me happy, I saw to it that no one was happy. You see I had all these great expectations of what our marriage would look like and what our children would be like.

My first problem was putting unreasonably high expectations on my family. We are only human. No one is perfect and we all have flaws and weaknesses along with our strengths and gifts. I should have cultivated those strengths instead of being too quick to judge those imperfections.

If the weekend didn't go the way I planned, I would pout on the inside and take it out on those around me. My husband thought I was on my period more than just one week a month. I was determined not to have a marriage like my parents, which finally did end my senior year of high school. I thought all the years of nagging and correcting my husband were just grooming us for a better future. All I was really doing was being a controlling and manipulative wife that put her needs before her family. Wow! That was a hard sentence to choke out there.

When someone in your family, whether it is a spouse, child, parent or sibling, needs a change in their lives, you can't change them. Only God can do that! The best thing you can do is lift them up in prayer, daily. Even if it takes weeks, months, or years, don't stop praying for them!

Well, had I stopped to intercede for changes that needed to be made in me, instead of going about trying to change everyone else, I would have seen that I was the one needing the most change. I needed to give God back the control He once had. I only thought I had everything under control. I controlled everything from our money to our household rules and even our intimacy. (Girls, we all know there is a lot of power to be wielded there).

So with all the responsibility I felt I had, came a lot of pressure. A lot of pressure to get things right and when they didn't, I would quickly spiral into feeling like a failure.

We had just begun to get out of a really difficult season in our lives. I finished college and started a really stressful full time job which threw our kids into daycare, both while avoiding foreclosure on our home. Thank goodness, the Lord saw us through!

We had made a real bad habit of calling on the Lord when things were tough, but not when things were fine. It was a "give me this, I need that" relationship. God wanted me to continue spending daily time with Him in His presence like I had so many years ago. I had forsaken that part of my life and was unable to hear His still, small voice because I didn't recognize it anymore.

Even so, the Lord was faithful and never, ever left me. I was able to quit that job, get a much better position, family-wise, at our church preschool and get our kids back out of daycare. Our finances were back to normal and the "almost foreclosure" mess was over. I could breathe, right? Well, I went through a rollercoaster of emotions during that time. I felt like I messed up with our money, therefore making me responsible for the near-foreclosure event.

One spring my husband left on a business trip and that first night when I was going to sleep, I felt like the wind got knocked out of me. I became overwhelmed with a spirit of worry, fear, anxiety and the feeling that I was alone. I was scared, nervous and didn't understand what was happening. I couldn't sleep or eat. I felt like all my confidence was gone in who I was and who

God was, and doubt made its home in my heart. A lot of people would refer to this as a panic or anxiety attack. All I knew was it felt foreign, strange, and scary.

First, I wanted to explain it and figure it out. I thought, *there is something wrong with me and I need to fix this.* So I convinced myself and everyone else that I was in need of some medical advice and thought perhaps it was a hormonal issue. I went to the doctor and he agreed with me. He changed my birth control pill, told me to exercise, and gave me an anti-anxiety pill for when I was having a really bad day.

I came home and everything inside of me felt empty, nearly in a state of despair. The news did not make me feel better at all. My mom suffered from some of these same issues when she was younger, and my grandmother also. So you can only imagine the field day Satan had with me thinking I was under some generational strongholds.

In my heart and in my spirit, I knew that there was only one answer, one fix, and one way to get out of this mess. I kept somewhat suppressing it due to the fact I thought it was purely medical and not spiritual. I knew God wanted me to be still and know that He was taking care of this and to trust Him, but I let other's peoples voices drown out His. I worked myself up into such a state one day in early April, I took my first anti-anxiety pill, against everything inside of me. I had a terrible reaction to it that night and my body did everything it could to get the pill out of my system. I ended up in the emergency room for dehydration. The doctor came in and told me "I don't know why that happened. You are perfectly healthy. Apparently your body did not want that pill and it wanted it out."

That afternoon I told God, *Okay, Lord you are bigger than any pill, any medical need, and I need you to help me trust in you for this. I can't explain why this is happening but you see the bigger picture here. I want to stop figuring it out and trying to explain it and let you work in this mess.*

I called and had a good friend pray for me. She said something to me that I will never forget. She said, "Perhaps this is just apart of your awesome testimony." What? I never thought of myself as having one. I never did drugs, had cancer, or any drastic sin, I thought. But I realized I didn't need to go through any of that stuff to be an overcomer. I had a different testimony.

I knew not everyone could relate to me, but there were a lot of people out there that just learned to cope with their depression and anxiety, I for one wanted to beat it! God already won this victory for me on the cross. I wanted to learn how to walk in it! I began to get a new perspective on my whole situation. I thought, *perhaps, something I am going though will encourage someone else one day.*

Now, I am not perfect but I am daily drawing near to God and learning to completely trust in Him for my family and for myself. Every storm we go through in life brings something we need. What is that? Rain! When we are dry we need God's word to saturate our roots like nothing else. It is important to note here that we should not allow ourselves to get dry in the first place. God spoke to me about what might look like my "yo-yo" relationship with Him and spoke something very powerful into my heart. *Michelle, I don't want to be your medicine for when you get sick. I want to be your daily regimen, like a multivitamin that keeps you healthy.* When I began to let God work this truth in me, my sleep came back, my appetite came back, and my peace came back.

Putting the Armor Back On

When I thought I was nothing, God saw a woman that was beautiful inside; strong, courageous, fearless and brave. That is not what I saw at the time, but as I began to align my vision with His, little bits of that woman came out. My flesh wars against the change, even now, and Satan tries to make me take two steps back when I take a huge step forward. But I know that when my God is for me, no weapon formed against me shall stand.

I remembered the dream I had as a little girl, and that if the devil can make you think you are weak or inadequate then he will keep you from accomplishing your purpose and your calling. If he can get you distracted with something else or even on something that's not true, then it keeps your focus off of what it's suppose to be on.

One of the most vital components of my restoration was remembering to put on my armor daily. Let's dive in to see exactly what this armor is that I am talking about.

"Finally, be strong in the Lord and in his mighty power. Put on the full armor of God so that you can take your stand against the devil's schemes. For our struggle is not against flesh and blood, but against the rulers, against the authorities, against the powers of this dark world and against the spiritual forces of evil in the heavenly realms. Therefore put on the full armor of God, so that when the day of evil comes, you may be able to stand your ground, and after you have done everything, to stand. Stand firm then, with the belt of truth buckled around your waist, with the breastplate of righteousness in place, and with your feet fitted with the readiness that comes from the gospel of peace. In addition to all this, take up the shield of faith, with which you can extinguish all the flaming arrows of the evil one. Take the helmet of salvation and the sword of the Spirit, which is the word of God. And pray in the Spirit on all occasions with all kinds of prayers and requests. With this in mind, be alert and always keep on praying for all the saints." Ephesians 6:10-18

When I was going through that battle with anxiety, my mom looked me in the eyes and said, "You don't have to take the hard road I did. I didn't know about the spiritual warfare being waged over me until much later in life. You know about the weapons of warfare at your disposal...use them!"

Those words stayed with me and I began to seek God for my purpose, my healing, and my future. But, I knew I had to go through His way, His word, His Holy Spirit and use His tools clearly laid out for me in Ephesians. I so badly wanted a more in depth look at each of these weapons. I wanted to know how they worked and what they protected.

I began to feel a stirring in me about looking deeper into each piece of armor, and to share what I learn along the way with you. I hope that together we will discover the mighty weapons God gives us in His word. Together we can equip ourselves to face whatever circumstance, illness, relationship, insecurity or situation might arise. I hope that you will be encouraged to "fight the good fight of faith" 1 Timothy 6:12.

Perhaps you are unfamiliar with God's word and the fact that there is even a spiritual realm at all. Perhaps it might seem a bit unnerving to you and even frightening. Well let me encourage you dear friends:

> "So do not fear, for I am with you; do not be dismayed, for I am your God. I will strengthen you and help you; I will uphold you with my righteous right hand" Isaiah 41:10.

Let's tap into this incredible source of strength and power right at our fingertips! Grab your Bible and dust it off if you

My Battle

need to. Let's discover the incredible calling on our lives and the mercy and grace our Heavenly father gives us daily.

Satan is not omnipresent, so he sends out his demons to trick and trap us into sin and negative thinking. I believe each one of those evil beings has a name like doubt, worry, confusion, fear, anxiety, depression, homosexuality, alcoholism, adultery, addiction, and so forth. Let's be aware of Satan's schemes, recognize our vulnerabilities and insecurities, and get ready to face the battle that rages over our hearts, minds, souls, and families. Let's take back what is ours! Let us claim together: "But we are not of those who shrink back and are destroyed, but of those who believe and are saved" Hebrews 10: 39.

2

The Shield of Faith

"...take up the shield of faith, with which you can extinguish all the flaming arrows of the evil one"
Ephesians 6: 16

The very first piece of armor God began to deal with me about is the shield of faith. I not only studied it, I lived it! Wouldn't you know that before this chapter is even written, my faith would have been tested. I began second-guessing this whole idea, and that I was even in a position worthy of revealing the awesome power of faith, let alone putting it in a book! But, as if I could hear the dings on my shield when I dodged an arrow, I knew God wanted me to do this. I would be encouraged from a reader on my blog or read an inspiring devotion somewhere and I would think God was trying to motivate me to keep my eyes fixed on Him and not on my shortcomings or weaknesses.

So what is this faith I speak of? It is explained in Hebrews 11:1 as "...being sure of what we hope for and certain of what we do not see". Faith is believing in someone or believing for something. The kind of faith I will speak of is faith in God and faith that Jesus Christ is His son. I believe that Jesus came to Earth and died for our sins. He rose again in three days and joined His father up in heaven to get our home ready to join Him one day. All we have do is ask for Him to come into our lives, take the reins, and live a life empowered by God's Holy Spirit and an abundance of grace.

One of the most incredible things about our Savior is that not only is He a kind, just and compassionate God, but He knows us inside and out. He came to Earth as a man and was tempted in every way we are tempted. He went through some of the exact situations and circumstances we have lived through or live in now.

Jesus Christ is relatable! The sooner we can realize that, the better off we will be. Do not be intimidated by His holiness. Do not fear a relationship with Christ because you think your sin has taken you to a point of no return. No, God is merciful and understanding! He wants nothing more than for us to take our mistakes, our mess, and our fears and turn them over to Him. Then when people can see the incredible change in our hearts and in our lives, they can see the true glory of God shining through.

"For it is by grace you have been saved, through faith-and not by works, so that no one can boast" says Ephesians 2:8. This scripture references that through our faith in the unseen but very present God, and the working of the Holy Spirit in our life, we can truly overcome anything that we need to.

Know Your Enemy

As much as we believe that there is a God who loves us, there is also an enemy who hates us. He is a thief of joy, peace, and stability. He wants to shake us up and tear us down. He will whisper lies that can even be disguised as our own voice.

Anything that isolates you from doing the will of God, whether it be in relationships or ministries, pray about it. Ask God to give you a spirit of discernment and pray 1 John 4:1-2 as you seek to clarify confusion you may have in any area of your life. The bible tells us to test the spirits and the wisdom God gives will be "pure, peace-loving, considerate, submissive, full of mercy and good fruit, impartial and sincere" James 3:17. We need to learn to recognize our insecurities, our weaknesses, or in other words, our most vulnerable spots in our armor.

In Isaiah 54:17 it says, "no weapon forged against you shall prevail, and you will refute every tongue that accuses you." Let's look at this verse in two different sections here.

First of all, look at the word forged. Forged means to form and fashion. I love the Merriam-Webster's dictionary definition, "to make or imitate falsely especially with intent to defraud" (4). So Satan is busy working all day to make an arrow with our name on it that will really hit us where it hurts: our finances, our marriage, our children and our friendships. He will bring back memories of failures and old thought patterns, and harmful mindsets.

Satan and his little demons are working overtime to make sure that we will doubt our abilities in ourselves and in our Lord. I don't tell you this to beware but to be aware! We need to know our enemy inside and out, how he works, and be aware of when we might be vulnerable to his attacks. We can grab our bibles and get down on our knees to ask God to help us raise our shield of faith at the right moment to deflect Satan's arrows.

H.A.L.T.

My grandmother, who I love and admire for her strength and courage and vast knowledge of God's word, told me something I will never forget. She said, "when you are going through spiritual warfare, remember the word H.A.L.T. When you feel the devil is really trying to mess with you, halt and think if you are **H**ungry, **A**ngry, **L**onely or **T**ired." These are all basic moments of weakness for all of us. Anytime I felt I was having a really bad day and knew my attitude was not where it should be and felt that it was taking its toll on me or my family, I would stop and think about whether I was any of these.

If I were hungry, I would eat. But I would be mindful of what I was eating and not just eat mindlessly (well talk more about this later).

If I were angry, I would try to make amends with that person before bedtime. If I were unable to, I'd pray about it asking God to not let bitterness or unforgiveness harbor in my heart.

If I were lonely, which would happen a lot when my husband was on business trips, I just asked God to give me a new mindset. I was never really alone I knew God was with me and I could call on Him anytime I wanted. I also had my children with me, so I tried to make that week be about them and focusing on some quality time with them. I also made an effort to get together with friends I didn't see much, not validating my fear of being alone, but in knowing that healthy, Christian relationships with other women were good for me.

If I were tired, then I would acknowledge it. I learned that admitting you are weary physically, mentally, or emotionally is not a weakness. It is healthy to acknowledge when you have had enough and ask for help from your husband with the kids, or if you need to get away for a couple of days on a vacation. You need to make your needs known to your family and to God. Matthew 11:28 says, "Come to me all you who are weary and burdened and I will give you rest."

Don't give the devil a foothold in any area of your life. "Do not be overcome by evil, but overcome evil with good" Romans 12:21.

I tell you this not to be fearful, but to be faith-full! When we wake up in the morning we need to ask God to help us lift our shields of faith and keep them lifted!

"Keep a cool head. Stay alert. The Devil is poised to pounce, and would like nothing better than to catch you napping. Keep your guard up. You're not the only ones plunged into these hard times. It's the same with Christians all over the world. So keep a firm grip on the faith. The suffering won't last forever. It won't be long before this generous God who has great plans for us in Christ—eternal and glorious plans they are! —will have you put together and on your feet for good. He gets the last word; yes, he does."
1 Peter 5:8-11 (MSG).

In the book of Matthew, it lays out the temptation of Jesus. Jesus had been fasting for forty days and nights and he was probably hungry and tired. Being in such a weak state physically, probably had an impact on Him mentally also.

Well, wouldn't you know this would be Satan's prime opportunity for attack? Because Satan is a coward! He waits until we are down for the count before he pounces. What kind of success do you think he would have if we were standing tall on the promises of God's word and claiming scripture over our minds and hearts? Not much. When we are at our weakest or most insecure we need to be on guard, lifting our shields against anything that would distract us from achieving victory.

Ever heard that old saying, "When it rains, it pours?" In one day you might have been late to work, while forgetting your lunch at home, missing that parent teacher conference in the afternoon and come home to dinner guests when you forgot to take the chicken out to thaw the night before.

Don't you think that just might put you on the edge? The edge I am talking about here is the edge of losing your joy, peace, and your sanity for the day. So what if, instead, we stopped at the end of that day and said, *Lord, today is rough and everything seems to be coming against me all at once. Help me to keep my cool and put my trust in you. I will trust that this day will get better, I would have much rather sat in traffic than actually been in the accident that caused it. I also trust that although my dinner wasn't home cooked you opened the door for me to minister to a couple that really needed it...even if it was over some Taco Bell.*

There is a lot going on in the spiritual realm we don't know about. When we make an intentional effort to commit our day to him and put our trust in His leading, he will "make your righteousness shine like the dawn, the justice of your cause like the noonday sun" Psalm 37:5.

Faith-Stealers

There are several different areas in our lives that can really test our faith. Let's look at just a couple and see if we can identify a specific area that we may not realize is stealing our faith.

The Shield of Faith

Worry- Well this is obviously a no- brainer right? Not exactly, worry is something we come into contact with much more than we think. We worry about our bills, our jobs, or the lack thereof. We worry about our health, children, marriage, and weight. We worry about important elections and even the weather forecast. The news and magazines don't help. Numerous media outlets that bombard us of everything negative constantly feed into our worrying. You have to look with a magnifying glass, it seems, to find something positive.

Worrying distracts us from trusting. If we give the Lord, daily, our concerns over all of these different things, then we can trust that He will take care of them. Proverbs 3:5-6 says, "Trust in the Lord with all your heart and lean not on your own understanding; in all your ways acknowledge him and He will make your paths straight." God asks us to give Him these issues and stop burdening ourselves with putting the whole world on our shoulders. When we can enter His rest and truly begin to trust Him to work in our life, we can really learn to let go and let God take control.

Sometimes, He asks us to do nothing. For many people, especially me, that is an extremely difficult task. I am a person that likes to be in control and monitor the situation. But as I have mentioned before, when you carry such a huge responsibility it heavily weighs on you when things begin to fall apart.

Matthew 6: 27 says, "Who by worrying can add a single hour to his life?" This is something we all need to take to heart. Does worrying solve the problem? No, every single time it makes things worse. When your mind is consumed with worry it affects not only you but also others around you. Loved ones notice the worry on your face and in your eyes. Does worry add more hours to your day to help you solve the problem? Quite the opposite in fact, it steals hours from your life! Worry can weigh a spirit down to a pit that is difficult to get out of, which leads me to the next faith-stealer.

Fear/Anxiety- I have a beautiful plaque hanging on my mantle that says, "There is no room for fear where there is faith." I bought it when I was suppose to go on stage and sing the solo in a choir special about two years ago.

I love to sing! I have been singing in church from my grade school years and all the way up to college. It is a passion of mine and I know without a doubt that God has called me to minister in song. I have led songs in worship, sang several choir specials, performed at weddings and funerals, and even competed in contests and festivals winning awards. But I have had to fight my fears the whole way through.

I dealt with severe performance anxiety my whole life until recently. I will lose my breath, my vision goes black, and my knees want to nearly come out from underneath me and most often when I am about to minister in church with a very powerful song. Well, why do you think that could be? If Satan could convince me that I couldn't do it and make me believe that perhaps the song isn't quite in my vocal range or perhaps I'll forget the words or that everyone will judge me, then I would become paralyzed with fear.

Fear and anxiety go hand in hand, ultimately one precedes the other. When I began to recognize the attacks, I would retreat quietly and ask the Lord to give me strength to minister through the song and help me to focus on Him. God was there for me every time. There is never a moment when He doesn't come through for us, we just have to ask.

Earlier when I talked about the anxiety/dehydration bout that landed me in the hospital, my husband's stepfather said something to me I will never forget. He came over before we had gone to the hospital to take care of my boys and I noticed he kept staring at me. Later he explained he had never seen someone so full of fear. He had been in the Vietnam War and seen men die and fear for their life and the look in my eyes reminded him of that when he looked in mine.

I had allowed my fear of the unknown and anxiety from too much worry put me in a position of all my faith being stripped away. I lost faith in myself and in God. It was a very dark place that I will never allow myself to go again. Even though I felt like giving up, God didn't give up on me. He was pursuing me back to a place of trust and faith in Him and all I needed to do was take a stand of faith for myself.

In Romans 12, it explains that God gives to each of us a measure of faith. How do we receive that faith? "...Faith comes from hearing the message, and the message is heard through the word of Christ" Romans 10:17. What Satan meant to harm me with, God used it for His glory. I get excited just writing that! I am thankful that through my faith, I was able to listen to what God wanted me to hear through His word.

He then filled me with trust, confidence, hope, love, and faith. He taught me how to lift my shield of faith by submerging myself in the awesome depths of His Holy Word and the freedom it gave.

Hall of Faith

In Hebrews 11, it lists several examples of people in the Bible that had great faith and believed in the promises God spoke to them. This passage is widely known as the "Hall of Faith". These people are not just characters in a story but real people that experienced miracles, received healing, and achieved great honor in the sight of God for their faith. As we look at a few of them, we may see a reflection of ourselves in their weaknesses, fears, and how they overcame with their faith.

Noah built a massive ark after God revealed to him that the Earth would be flooded and his family would be the sole survivors. So he obeyed and persevered despite ridicule and condemnation from his friends and neighbors. Imagine if he allowed his fear of rejection and ridicule keep him from accomplishing his task?

Abraham and Sarah were very old and way past their childbearing years, but knew that God wanted to use them to birth a nation. From this couple "...came descendants as numerous as the stars in the sky and as countless as the sand on the seashore" Hebrews 11:12. Imagine if they had they listened to the words of the doctors in those days that were baffled at their infertility instead of the great physician that had the power to heal?

Moses' parents knew there was something special about him as a baby. Instead of throwing him into the Nile, which was Pharaoh's orders for every Hebrew boy at the time, they put him in a basket in the Nile trusting that God would guard and protect him, leading him to safety and ultimately Israel's freedom.

In Matthew 17:20, Jesus explains "...if you have faith as small as a mustard seed, you can say to this mountain, 'Move from here to there' and it will move. Nothing will be impossible for you." Look at that last sentence. Nothing will be impossible for you! Wow! God wants us to have that kind of faith: the faith that can allow the impossible to become possible. Let's begin living that, and I dare you to see if your life doesn't change!

A Confident Faith

"Do not throw away your confidence; it will be richly rewarded. You need to persevere so that when you have done the will of God, you will receive what he has promised" Hebrews 10:35-36.

When I finished studying the book of Hebrews I noticed there was a recurrent theme in this incredible book of the Bible: confidence! It begins in the first several chapters explaining how Jesus is the new high priest and he has come to replace the old. It explains the old order of the Levitical priesthood was trumped by Jesus' much higher calling of establishing a new law, a new order and filling that gap between God and us. In Hebrews, it explains that Jesus' new covenant is founded on "better promises". I just love that!

In Hebrews 8:10, the Lord says that in this new covenant, "I will put my laws in their minds and write them on their hearts. I will be their God and they will be my people." This says that no longer will there be this separation for which a priest will need to shed an animals blood for repentance of sins. Jesus has already done all the shedding of blood there will ever be! So "we have confidence to enter the Most Holy Place by the blood of Jesus" Hebrews 10:19.

The Shield of Faith

"Let us then approach the throne of grace with confidence, so that we may receive mercy and find grace to help us in our time of need" Hebrews 4:16. Jesus has thrown the door open! We can rest at His feet, ask for wisdom, seek his guidance, praise His name, rejoice in his mercy, ask for forgiveness, and know with confidence that he hears us and we will receive what he has promised us.

So I looked up this word, confidence, and in all the different Bible translations and in dictionary definitions, I found these words: fearless, assurance, boldness, believing, trusting, and having no doubt. We as Christians need to stand firm on His promises, on His word, and be confident in the face of doubt.

We need to be confident in the face of fear, in the face of uncertainty, in the face of insecurity, in the face of unemployment, in the face of failed relationships, in the face of sickness, and in the face of mental strongholds. Anything that takes captive our God-given talents and abilities to reach our potential needs to be thrown away, not our confidence. Do not let other people's negativity or even your own negativity keep you from accomplishing all that you were created to be.

I went through a season where all my confidence felt stripped away. A few whispers of self-doubt from Satan and my mind was spinning. Instead of dismissing the lies, I considered them. Big mistake! I went into a tailspin of second-guessing myself, doubting that God could use me, and focusing on my weaknesses.

Instead I should have quoted with confidence what Hebrews 13:6 says, "The Lord is my Helper; I will not be seized with alarm [I will not fear or dread or be terrified]. What can man do to me?" We need to be aware that what Satan has used before to bring us down, he will try again. He nearly had me thinking that I was in relapse of old behaviors and thought patterns.

In my mind the negativity was screaming at me, but in the stillness of worship I heard God's sweet voice in my head. God was speaking to me that the doubts were all merely a distraction. If the devil can keep me from fixing my eyes on Jesus and instead focus all my efforts on myself and what is wrong with me, I cannot focus on what the Lord wants me to focus on.

God wants me to focus on my strengths. He wants me to focus on my future. He wants me to focus on fulfilling the callings of ministry placed in my life. Satan wants nothing more than to make an enemy of your circumstances, your spouse, your church, your family, and even yourself. If he can get you to believe lies of inadequacy, fear, doubt or worthlessness then you won't produce any fruit.

Get bold! Get courageous! Get fearless! Get confident! Hebrews 11:1 says, "Faith is being sure of what we hope for and certain of what we do not see". Believe Him for your healing, believe Him for your relationships, and believe Him for your future!

The Shield of Faith

I read all the examples Hebrews 11 gave of Noah, Abraham, Gideon, and Moses. Although all these people had trials and weaknesses, they persevered anyways and received what they were promised! So I wrote my own passage of faith. I will share a little bit with you:

- By faith, Michelle believed that God would use her to minister to other people inside and outside of her family. She believed her heart of compassion for other women to daily equip themselves with their armor would spread like wildfire, strengthening families and uniting the body of Christ to stand firm against the enemy's attacks.

- By faith, Michelle believed for financial miracles within her own finances and to get to the place where paying for things with cash and not having to use credit would become the norm, not the exception.

- By faith, Michelle would intercede on behalf of her children to grow up under a Godly influence, be able to decipher the difference between light and dark, and be a light shining for God!

- By faith, Michelle believed that relationships within her family would be completely restored and peace would rule in the homes of other family members.

Sit down, read Hebrews 11, be inspired and write your own "passage of faith". Believe God for it, pray about it, and be confident that God will hear you. Then go ahead and thank God for what He is going to do. Receive it and claim it!

Oil the Shields!

Several different passages in the Bible, share a common theme when it comes to picking up your shield for battle.

- "Get up you officers, oil the shields!" Isaiah 21:5

- "For there the shield of the mighty was defiled...no longer rubbed with oil." 2 Samuel 1:21

- "Prepare your shields, both large and small, and march out for battle!" Jeremiah 46:3

In the King James Version of Isaiah 21:5 it replaces "oil the shields" with "anointing the shields." It was believed to help make the shields more slippery so that the arrows of the enemy might bounce off more easily. When we walk out into the battlefield we need to make sure that our shields of faith are anointed!

As I was reading about confidence in Hebrews, as referenced above, I heard the Lord speak to me that the oil on my shield of faith needed to be confidence. I needed to be confident in my faith, confident in his ability to work out my situations for

The Shield of Faith

good, and confident that he was going to use my flaws and all to minister to those around me as He in turn ministered to me through His word and Holy Spirit.

Lift Your Shields

In the book of Matthew it tells of all the miracles and healings Jesus did. There was healings of demon possession, blind eyes being opened, and even the dead being brought back to life.

In each of these instances, Jesus would say, "Your faith has healed you" or "By your faith, you have been healed". The people seeking healing believed that through one touch of his robe or one word spoken from his lips they would be healed. They had to believe without a trace of fear or doubt in their hearts and minds that the healing they were seeking would be done.

In Matthew, chapter 17, it tells an account of when the disciples tried to heal a boy who was possessed but they had no success. So they brought him to Jesus and he rebuked the evil spirit and sent it fleeing. The disciples asked Jesus why they were unable to drive it out and Jesus replied, "Because you have so little faith. I tell you the truth, if you have faith as small as a mustard seed, you can say to this mountain. 'Move from here to there' and it will move. Nothing will be impossible for you" Matthew 17:20.

When we are in need of deliverance we need to boldly come before God, with confidence that He will hear us and our faith will melt His heart and He will respond with love and restoration. Psalm 34:17-20 says:

"The righteous cry out, and the Lord hears them; he delivers them from all their troubles. The Lord is close to the brokenhearted and saves those who are crushed in spirit. A righteous man may have many troubles but the Lord delivers him from them all; he protects all his bones; not one of them will be broken."

Amen! Did you read that? Read it again! If you are lacking in confidence, all you have to do is read this and your faith will strengthen tenfold. When we cry out to God, he hears us and delivers us from not one of our troubles, or a few of them, but ALL of them!

What does it mean by saying "those who are crushed in spirit"? Those who have a spirit of heaviness or despair, those who have a spirit of depression looming or any yokes of oppression...He will save you! We will all have issues and drama but He will deliver us and in the process not one of our bones will be broken!

We may feel like we are in a million little pieces by the time the day is over but when we give those pieces to God, He puts together something that was even more beautiful than what He started with.

Shield of Togetherness

In my study of the shield of faith, I began to do some study into how it relates to an actual piece of armor like that of the Roman soldier. The Roman shields, or scutum, were about three and a half feet tall and almost three feet wide. These shields were large enough to cover nearly the entire body when they were ready for battle.

An amazing battle formation the Roman soldiers would make, is to form a line that was four men wide and four men deep. Those on the outer edges would turn their shields out and those in the middle would turn their shields up. This would make a nearly impenetrable line of defense. We can become a powerful force to be reckoned with when we come together as believers and intercede with and for each other.

During a difficult period in my life, our church began a Tuesday evening bible study. It was a different format than what I was used to. Normally, we had Beth Moore studies with a video, but our women's director had it put on her heart to just study scripture and have an open floor discussion time.

It was incredible to see not only me, but many different women come out of our shells and grow spiritually, emotionally, and in our knowledge of God's word. The older women had incredible testimonies that inspired me. Women of other cultures told stories of perseverance despite their family's objections and younger women shared their hungry heart for more of God.

It's funny how God gives us just what we need right when we need it. He knew that during that time in my life I needed that. He knew that I needed to have an outlet for me to pour out what He was pouring in. During the times that I felt dry, He would fill me through words of encouragement, advice, or scripture that we would study for that evening.

When someone had a prayer need, we would lay hands and pray for healing, restoration, guidance or whatever the issue was. You could almost feel the gates of heaven open up and the demons flee the area when we would come together and pray for someone. I loved it!

Now I know that not everyone has that. Perhaps you are in a situation where your church family has burned you. Perhaps you don't go to church at all. I encourage you to ask the Lord to bring God-fearing and supportive women into your life. Women that will encourage you and when you confide in them, will lift your needs to the Lord in prayer on your behalf.

Be wary of those that take what you share and share it with everyone they know. Don't be around gossips! Ask God to give you discernment and wisdom to know who to share your needs with or who you yourself could be a blessing to.

There is ample evidence in scripture that supports the need for togetherness. Let's look at a few of these:

- Leviticus 26:7-8 - (The Lord spoke to Moses on Mt. Sinai) "...You will pursue your enemies, and they will fall by the sword before you. Five of you will chase a hundred, and a hundred of you will chase ten thousand..."

- Deuteronomy 32:30 - (Moses is singing a song of praise unto the Lord and referring to the Lord as "The Rock") "...How could one man chase a thousand, or two put ten thousand to flight, unless their Rock had sold them, unless the Lord had given them up?"

- Matthew 18:19 - "...I tell you that if two of you on earth agree about anything you ask for, it will be done for you by my Father in Heaven. For where two or three come together in my name, there am I with them."

- Ephesians 4:2; 4: 11-13 - "Be completely humble and gentle; be patient, bearing with one another in love... It was he who gave some to be apostles, some to be prophets, some to be evangelists, some to be pastors and teachers, to prepare God's people for works of service, so that the body of Christ may be built up until we all reach unity in the faith and in the knowledge of the Son of God and become mature, attaining to the whole measure of the fullness of Christ."

- Hebrews 10:25 - "Let us not give up meeting together, as some are in the habit of doing, but let us encourage one another- and all the more as you see the Day approaching."

- James 5:16 - Therefore confess your sins to each other and pray for each other so that you may be healed. The prayer of a righteous man is powerful and effective.

Let's remember to lift our shields when doubt and fear wants to prevail. When you believe for that financial miracle, that healing for your friend, or the salvation of a loved one, do not neglect the powerful piece of armor that is at use for our disposal- faith. When we remember to put it on daily, faith releases the impossible to become possible, the dream to become the reality and the destroyer to cower in our shadow.

At the end of each chapter, I will put a section entitled, "Arm Yourself". This will be a portion of scriptures that pertain to each piece of armor as we go through them. Read them, meditate on them, and pray them over yourself. Nothing is more powerful than applying scripture to your life and circumstances. Ask the Lord to take you deeper in to this area and be blessed in your heart, mind and spirit.

Arm Yourself

- "In His great mercy He has given us new birth into a living hope through the resurrection of Jesus Christ from the dead, and into an inheritance that can never perish, spoil or fade- kept in heaven for you, who through faith are shielded by God's power until the coming of the salvation that is ready to be revealed in the last time. In this you greatly rejoice, though now for a little while you may have had to suffer grief in all kinds of trial. These have come so that your faith- of greater worth than gold, which perishes even though refined by fire- may be proved genuine and may result in praise, glory and honor when Jesus Christ is revealed." 1 Peter 1: 3-7

- "Be self controlled and alert. Your enemy the devil prowls around like a roaring lion looking for someone to devour. Resist him, standing firm in the faith, because you know that your brothers throughout the world are undergoing the same kind of sufferings." 1 Peter 5:8-9

- "...make every effort to add to your faith goodness; and to goodness, knowledge; and to knowledge, self-control; and to self-control, perseverance; and to perseverance, godliness; and to godliness, brotherly kindness; and to brotherly kindness, love." 2 Peter 1:5-7

- "But you dear friends, build yourselves up in your most holy faith and pray in the Spirit." Jude 1:20

- "Be on your guard; stand firm in the faith; be men of courage; be strong." 1 Corinthians 16:13

- "Though you have not seen Him, you love Him; and even though you do not see Him now, you believe in Him are filled with an inexpressible and glorious joy, for you are receiving the goal of your faith, the salvation of your souls." 1 Peter 1:8-9

3

The Belt of Truth

*"Stand firm then, with the belt of truth
buckled around your waist..."*
Ephesians 6:14

This next piece of armor is vital. It can be difficult to weed through what is truth and what is a lie. For many years, I believed that whatever thought plopped into my head, couldn't be helped, and it was what I felt. I thought I just needed to give in. I believed fighting it would be harder, only to find out that living in the daily bondage of being a slave to my thoughts, good and bad, is no way to live.

Not everything I think about my family, my job, my circumstances, or even myself is correct. I allowed myself to be ruled by my feelings, which then wreaked havoc on my emotions and then made me a miserable person to live with. The ones we love most are often times the ones that have to put up with the worst of us.

If you couple that with the hormonal issues we women deal with, you better watch out. MomWifeWomanZilla is on the loose! I have learned that at those lovely, crucial times of the month, to not allow myself to make any big decisions. Everything is amplified times ten whether it is good or bad during those very vulnerable moments.

When we give God full access into the deepest, darkest emotions and feelings and give Him the control of our emotional rollercoaster, the ride suddenly turns smoother. Life will naturally come with its own dips and dives. But, with that belt of His truth buckled around our waist we are less likely to be thrown about and rattled to our core.

Unfortunately, many of us have taken what others have said to us in the past and allowed it to become our current truth and our reality. When negative words and even abusive words or actions have come into our lives at a young or old age, we need to take action! We need to replace those lies with scriptures that feed into our soul, comfort our spirit, and give peace to our hearts and minds. Philippians 4: 8 says, "Finally brothers whatever is true, whatever is noble, whatever is right, whatever is pure, whatever is lovely, whatever is admirable- if anything is excellent or praiseworthy-think about such things."

Let's break this down a bit. First, it says whatever is true, noble, and right. This means we need to get rid of the deceptions and lies Satan has fed into our lives over the years. Let's ask God to help us take a step back and see ourselves through His eyes, not our own.

The second part says to think on what is pure, lovely, and admirable. This means we need to ask God to align our vision with His. We can't see the future, but God knows what we are capable of, even when we can't see it yet. God knows our potential and we need to ask Him to help us focus on our strengths and take advantage of the open doors and opportunities He sends our way. We need to get our minds off of ourselves and our pasts, failures and shortcomings and gain a new perspective. We need to ask God to help us see those pure, lovely, and admirable traits and characteristics that we can't see on our own.

Lastly, Paul said for us to think about anything excellent or praiseworthy. A great piece of advice to follow is found in Romans 12:21 which says, "Do not be overcome with evil, but overcome evil with good." An excellent way to overcome injustice done to us in the past and lies we've believed for so long is making up our minds to change our minds.

Decide today that you are done with the poor self-confidence, the self-doubt, the fear, or whatever you may be facing. Starting today, begin to proclaim the future is in your favor and that you can do anything with God's help. Decide today that you won't give up on yourself, because God surely has not given up on you.

You are still here! You still have a purpose and until you draw that last breath, every day is a brand new day to get it right, make it right, and live it right! Jesus came so that we might have life to the most full. Let's give it back to Him and allow His Holy Spirit and Word to transform us into what we were created to be.

Truth

Truth is what we believe to be our reality. There are two different kinds of truth to look at here. One is perceived truth and the other actual truth. Let's delve into both of them.

Perceived truth is the mental image of ourselves. It is molded from our past experiences, the good and the bad, and helps to mold our personalities and some of our character traits. If we grew up in a loving home that never tasted the bitterness of divorce, then we may grow up to have a strong sense of family and security. If we didn't we might have feelings of abandonment or commitment issues.

Maybe we grew up in a home full of healthy food and parents that put priority on making healthy choices and exercise. Then we are likely to grow up with a broad range of healthy eating habits and a fit lifestyle. If we did not, we may suffer with eating disorders and unhealthy self images that have in turn allowed ourselves to become physically unhealthy. I don't mean to stereotype here, just throwing out some scenarios that show how perception in what we believe to be our truth can quickly become skewed by learned behaviors and authority figures in our lives.

It is not always our parent's faults though. Perhaps we have faced some previous hurts from other family members or friends. Maybe a school bully did a lot of damage in those four years of high school that you thought no amount of positive words could ever repair. The perception we have of ourselves can become deeply rooted with good and bad. Unfortunately, these roots eventually do begin to produce fruit in our lives.

In Matthew 13, Jesus tells of the Parable of the Weeds. Here he explains of a man who sowed seeds of wheat. While he was sleeping, the man's enemy came and sowed seeds of weeds among the wheat. The weeds and the wheat grew together and at the proper time the man gathered the weeds, bundled it and burned it. He then gathered the wheat and harvested it and stored it in his barn.

This parable relates to the fact that all of our lives we have had times when weeds and wheat grew together. When we open ourselves up to God's threshing floor, He then begins to deal with us about the weeds in our lives that do not belong and brings out the real harvest of strong, healthy wheat. This is the wheat we need to store up and use, cultivate, knead and develop in to something great that God had planned for us all along.

Actual truth is the facts in our lives, or as I call them the labels. Let's take a look at some of these:

- Cancer survivor

- Alcoholic

- Abuser

- Victim

- Drug Addict

- Divorcee

- Bi-Polar

These labels are what we live with, grow up with, and too often we allow these to define us. Let's look at these labels as just names. But there is a name above all names. In 1 John 4:4 it explains that we are from God and have overcome (these labels) because the one who is in us is greater than the one who is in the world.

Our pasts have modeled and shaped our perspective and temperament but we decide how we will react to our current problems today. If we have acted poorly in the past, we can ask for forgiveness from God and others but it is important that we move on. Our actual truth can at times look bleak and the odds may seem stacked against us. If we allow God to work on our behalf to shape our circumstances for a greater testimony and outcome He will do it!

Pushing through our Past

As a young girl, I was filled with insecurities that I carried deep inside of me. I always felt I wasn't good enough to have good things. I thought there wasn't anything that special about me. I didn't begin to change that mindset until I realized that I could have a different mindset.

The Belt of Truth

I began to allow God to whisper the beautiful truth in my ear that He wanted me to hear. I never heard it spoken more beautifully to me than when I recently read an incredible book by Renee Swope called *A Confident Heart.* In it she says:

> "When doubt washes over me, often it is because something has happened to trigger my old emotions and create thoughts in my mind that are similar to those I had as a child. Sometimes that hurt little girl still has too much to say in my heart, if I listen to her powerful, yet immature emotions from my past rise to the surface. But they are not truth in my life. The insecurities are not the truth in your life either. As we look at our doubts and develop confident hearts, it's going to be important to recognize negative emotions from our past that keep us from living confidently in our present and future." (2)

After reading that I dropped to the floor and cried. I had never realized how much power I gave that little girl, even in my adult life. I decided that day and from then on to do everything I could to shut that little girl up! I asked God to help me deal with any old issues together and never again miss out on an opportunity for growth out of fear or insecurity.

How much power are you giving your past over your present life? Stop and ask God to begin showing you areas where Satan has smeared you with lies and begin to let God's truth really soak in.

Lies

Satan's primary weapon is lies. After all he is the father of lies. Let's look at what John 8:44 says, "...the devil...was a murderer from the beginning, not holding to the truth, for there is no truth in him. When he lies, he speaks his native language, for he is a liar and the father of lies." It is not possible for Satan to speak truth. He cannot and he is sly at filling your head with thoughts that are discouraging, depressing, full of fear, and hateful.

In Revelation 12:10, it is explained that he stands before God, night and day, accusing us. How many of you have felt guilt, sorrow and hopelessness? How many people have believed his lies and turned their backs on our Lord? How many lives could have been saved if only they knew the lies being fed to them were not their actual truth but only a perception of their circumstances?

God is here with us and in us, wanting us to call out to Him and ask for His help which He is more than ready to give. Together I want us to uncover some lies that I believe need God's light shone on them.

Lie

There is no hope for someone like me.

Truth

"For I know the plans I have for you," declares the Lord, "plans to prosper you and not to harm you, plans to give you a hope and a future." Jeremiah 29:11.

Lie

I don't seem to fit in anywhere. What's the use?

Truth

"For you created my inmost being; you knit me together in my mother's womb. I praise you because I am fearfully and wonderfully made; your works are wonderful I know that full well. My frame was not hidden from you when I was made in the secret place. When I was woven together in the depths of the earth, your eyes saw my unformed body. All the days ordained for me were written in your book before one of them came to be" Psalm 139: 13-16.

Lie

I don't know if God could really use me.

Truth

"For we are God's workmanship, created in Christ Jesus to do good works, which God prepared for us in advance for us to do" Ephesians 2:10.

Lie

I am afraid I will relapse and ruin my witness.

Truth

"It is for freedom that Christ has set us free. Stand firm, then, and do not let yourselves be burdened again by a yoke of slavery" Galatians 5:1.

Lie

I'm too young to have a vision or ministry.

Truth

"Don't let anyone look down on you because you are young, but set an example for the believers in speech, in life, in love, in faith and in purity" 1 Timothy 4:12.

Lie

My circumstances are so difficult right now. I don't think it will ever get better.

Truth

"So we fix our eyes on not what is seen but what is unseen. For what is seen is temporary, but what is unseen is eternal" 2 Corinthians 4:18.

The Belt of Truth

Lie

I don't think I'll be ever to stop my (sin/depression/addiction, etc.)

Truth

"No temptation has seized you except what is common to man. And God is faithful he will not let you be tempted beyond what you can bear. But when you are tempted, he will also provide a way out so that you can stand up under it" 1 Corinthians 10:13.

Lie

The Bible is irrelevant in today's society.

Truth

"For everything that was written in the past was written to teach us, so that through endurance and the encouragement of the Scriptures we might have hope" Romans 15:4.

These are only a handful of lies that are common. Perhaps you can relate to some of these or maybe you are dealing with a lie that isn't listed above. I implore you to pray about it and dig into God's word to find the truth you need to discover for that area in your life. Begin replacing the lies in your mind with His truth.

Arm Yourself

- "If you hold to my teaching, you are really my disciples. Then you will know the truth, and the truth will set you free" John 8:31-32.

- "Yet a time is coming and has now come when the true worshipers will worship the Father in the Spirit and in truth, for they are the kind of worshipers the Father seeks. God is spirit, and his worshipers must worship in the Spirit and in truth" John 4:23-24.

- "But when he, the Spirit of truth, comes, he will guide you into all the truth. He will not speak on his own; he will speak only what he hears, and he will tell you what is yet to come" John 16:13.

- "Jesus answered, "I am the way and the truth and the life. No one comes to the Father except through me" John 14:6.

- "You were running a good race. Who cut in on you to keep you from obeying the truth? That kind of persuasion does not come from the one who calls you. "A little yeast works through the whole batch of dough." I am confident in the Lord that you will take no other view. The one who is throwing you into confusion, whoever that may be, will have to pay the penalty" Galatians 5:7-10.

4

The Helmet of Salvation

"Take the helmet of salvation..."
Ephesians 6: 17

The next piece of the armor is one that protects us from the deadliest blow. The helmet protects our minds. We need to first have faith in the one true and living God, believing that He died for us and redeemed us from our sins. Secondly, we need to tear down the walls of lies that have been built up over the years and begin to allow God's truth to penetrate our hearts. How are we to begin to make sense of all of this? To begin to allow our salvation from God to take root in the biggest battlefield of all...our mind!

When I first began to think about this particular piece of armor, I wanted to dive deeper to understand salvation and what that means. My initial thought process was that salvation meant that I believed in God and after asking Him into my heart, I was saved through God's supernatural and extraordinary grace. But I felt there was more to this, I was missing something.

I looked in the bible and found numerous passages linking our salvation as a defense and as our strength. I wanted to dive deeper into what these scriptures knew that I didn't. Let's look at a few of these examples:

- "The Lord is my rock, my fortress and my deliverer; my God is my rock, in whom I take refuge. He is my shield and the horn of my salvation, my stronghold" Psalm 18:2.

- The Lord is my strength and song; he has become my salvation" Psalm 118:14.

- "Surely God is my salvation; I will trust and not be afraid. The Lord, the Lord himself, is my strength and my defense; he has become my salvation" Isaiah 12:2.

In these examples it is clear that God is a safe place for us. A place where we can put our trust. He is someone we can go to and let our hair down, cry out our eyes, and share the deepest and darkest parts of ourselves. He knows the desire of our hearts anyways. He only wants us to vocalize those heartfelt prayers and needs so then He can go to work on our behalf.

Freedom

According to the Merriam Webster Dictionary, salvation is defined as 1) deliverance from the power and effects of sin, 2) liberation from...illusion, and preservation from... destruction (3). So salvation is our deliverance, liberation, and preservation.

The Helmet of Salvation

To me this means that salvation is the key to our freedom! Freedom to live in Christ! Freedom to live the more abundant life that He promises! Freedom to live with the confident faith we were meant to.

When Jesus died on the cross he took the weight of sin in our lives and carried it. When we ask the Lord to forgive us and help us to overcome and provide a way out, He does so! We no longer need to feel that we carry the weight on our shoulders. He did that for us already.

We are free on this earth to make our own choices and have our own freewill. That does not give us permission to continue in the same negative behavior patterns or thought patterns that led to sin in the first place. We need to ask God to help us make healthy decisions daily and choices that begin putting our feet in the right direction. Whether you are moving forward by leaps and bounds or baby steps, every step closer to God's will for your life is a step in the right direction.

Sin can carry with it the trap of bondage. If we believe that we are a slave to our sin, then we will be. If we believe that we will overcome, we can do that too. When we take that step of faith and ask the Lord to deliver us from our sin and set us free, we need to shut out any condemning thoughts that Satan may try to whisper. Romans 8: 1-2 explains, "Therefore there is now no condemnation for those who are in Christ Jesus, because through

Christ Jesus the law of the Spirit of life set me free from the law of sin and death."

There are days when it is hard. Even days when it seems like we have failed. I remember moments when I thought I was relapsing into anxiety or depression. I thought something was wrong with me and I must not be doing something right so I would fall down to my knees and ask God to forgive me for whatever I was doing wrong.

I remember crying to my husband about it one night, thinking I must have done something wrong for feeling like I was in some sort of relapse. He looked at me and said, "You haven't done anything wrong". Something really struck me from that one simple statement. I thought about whenever I was making some real progress in my spiritual journey. I would come into heavy opposition that would deceive me into thinking I had never truly made progress in the first place.

The next morning in my quiet time with God, I felt the Lord speaking to me, "This is just his tactic to distract you." If the enemy could get me so absorbed in myself and what was still wrong with me then I would be blinded to see the true progress I was making. If he could get my eyes off of God then I would become consumed with negative thoughts and old behaviors.

I had a very negative viewpoint of the Lord in that time of my life that I needed help changing. I used to think that in times

The Helmet of Salvation

like those, or when I felt I was having a bad day, or letting a poor attitude out or saying something hurtful, I thought God was disappointed in me. I actually believed He would immediately take away all blessing in my life and shun me from ever calling me to do ministry again. I would instantly feel unworthy of His love and assured myself that he was turning His back on me.

Lo and behold was I wrong! These were nothing but lies! God never changes! One thing I had to learn was that God loves me no matter what. My salvation never leaves me. God is not disappointed in me. He doesn't disown me because I am anxious and fearful of my past or future. I am not disqualified from having a bright future because of one bad day.

When I came to that realization, I felt my spirit soar. It also helped me to think about it the way I think about my children. If they are having a bad day, like attitude problems or behavior issues, I don't run out and say, "I give up and throw in the towel on this one." No, I love them through those days and moments. I encourage them and pray for them, just as the Holy Spirit does for us. Even the Holy Spirit prays on our behalf! Look at what Romans 8: 26-27 says:

> "In the same way, the Spirit helps us in our weakness. We do not know what we ought to pray for, but the Spirit himself intercedes for us through wordless groans. And he who searches our hearts knows the mind of the

Spirit, because the Spirit intercedes for God's people in accordance with the will of God."

Even when we don't know what to say or how to pray, we can just sit quietly in His presence and ask the Holy Spirit to intercede on our behalf. We know that he does so with the most eloquent of words as he searches our heart. With the realization that even at my worst He loves me and fights for me, He delivers me from all my enemies.

In Ephesians chapter three, it says we can come to the very throne room of God with freedom and confidence. This freedom comes in being assured of our salvation. With God being for us, who can possibly stand against us? Through salvation we have been delivered from our enemies, our past, and our sin. We need the Holy Spirit's help in walking in that victory daily. Through salvation, we are liberated from the illusions Satan tries to manipulate us with.

Finding our Identity in Christ

How do we preserve this salvation? How do we keep our helmets on? Well for one let's remember no one can take off our helmets unless we willingly hand them over. No one can take any of our pieces of armor without our permission first. So let's resolve from this day forward that no one will take from us our true identity, which is found in Christ.

The Helmet of Salvation

Our identity defines who we are. Being a Christian is not a learned behavior but it is a lifestyle. It should go with us wherever we go and be felt by everyone we meet. It should be evident by our actions and attitudes. It should govern what movies and television shows we watch. Being a follower of Christ should dictate the choices we make for mind, body, and soul.

Whatever we feed ourselves spiritually will eventually come out. So why not feed your soul God's word? The answers to life's biggest questions are in there. Questions like: Who am I? Why am I here? What purpose lies before me? How do I access these incredible truths for my life? Will I ever conquer my past? It's in there we just need to look for it.

Matthew 6: 20-21 says, "But store up for yourselves treasures in heaven, where moth and rust do not destroy, and where thieves do not break in and steal. For where your treasure is, there your heart will be also." What does a pirate or Indiana Jones do when there is a treasure to be found? They go full speed and at all costs until it is found! We need to have that same kind of passion to search for what God has for us in this life. We find that through Him and only Him. No one can tell us what we are suppose to accomplish for God's kingdom. No one can decide for us what path to take in this life. Only God can! I promise you if we ask Him, He will tell us.

We have not, because we ask not. Stop the excuses and thinking that it is too hard. I went through a period where I didn't want to know because maybe I wouldn't like what He would have to say. I believe it is harder to walk in disobedience than waltzing through the open doors and opportunities He opens for us. The only way we will know if we are heading in the right direction is if we are in close fellowship with Him.

If you are reading this with expectation that you should have your life all figured out by the end of this book or even this chapter, you've got it all wrong. If you think I am going to sit here and tell you what your identity is in Christ you are mistaken. I am here to share with you what God has put in *my* heart. I am called to share the knowledge of the armor that *I* have lived and experienced through my walks and talks with God. I hope that at the end of this book you are encouraged to pick up your armor and retake the battleground over your mind, heart, family and friends. I believe with increased knowledge comes increased responsibility to either choose to apply that knowledge to our daily lives or stick it back on the shelf and choose to go back to the way life was. So together let's look at how we are to identify our identity in Christ.

I believe there are two different parts to our identity: personal and kingdom. First, we will take a look at our personal identity in Christ. Let's read 2 Corinthians 12:12: "The body is a unit, though it is made up of many parts... they form one body." Our personal identity is what confirms if we are the leg, head, arm or foot in the body of Christ. We have a specific calling or gifting on our life, whether it be wisdom and knowledge, faith and obedience,

The Helmet of Salvation

healing, miracles, ability to prophesy, discernment between spirits, speaking in tongues, or the interpretation (see 1 Cor. 12:4-11). It is unique to our DNA. Our personal identity is how we are wired in our personality and disposition; it's what makes us special and sets us apart from everyone else.

Our kingdom identity is what we, as Christians, can all claim in our lives. It is clearly laid out for us in the bible and we need to begin claiming it, praying it, and receiving it in our lives. When we looked at the belt of truth, we talked about replacing Satan's lies with the truth of God's word. Well, here are some incredible truths we can fill our minds with and stand on. Each of these passages are from different bible translations so you can really read the real meat coming from each verse. I gave each scripture a positive label we can begin speaking over our lives as we meditate on the verse.

- **I am the King's daughter!** "This resurrection life you received from God is not a timid, grave-tending life. It's adventurously expectant, greeting God with a childlike "What's next, Papa?" God's Spirit touches our spirits and confirms who we really are. We know who he is, and we know who we are: Father and children. And we know we are going to get what's coming to us—an unbelievable inheritance! We go through exactly what Christ goes through. If we go through the hard times with him, then we're certainly going to go through the good times with him!" Romans 8:15-17 (MSG)

Arm Yourself

- **I am loved!** "But in all these troubles we have complete victory through God, who has shown his love for us. Yes, I am sure that nothing can separate us from God's love—not death, life, angels, or ruling spirits. I am sure that nothing now, nothing in the future, no powers, nothing above us or nothing below us—nothing in the whole created world—will ever be able to separate us from the love God has shown us in Christ Jesus our Lord." Romans 8:37-39 (ERV)

- **I know that God hears me!** "Let us then fearlessly *and* confidently *and* boldly draw near to the throne of grace (the throne of God's unmerited favor to us sinners), that we may receive mercy [for our failures] and find grace to help in good time for every need [appropriate help and well-timed help, coming just when we need it." Hebrews 4:16 (AMP)

- **I am alive with his Spirit!** "I will put my Spirit in you, and you will come to life again. Then I will lead you back to your own land. Then you will know that I am the LORD. You will know that I said this and that I made it happen.'" This is what the LORD said." Ezekiel 37:14 (ERV)

- **I am light in this dark world!** "We heard the true teaching from God. Now we tell it to you: God is light, and in him there is no darkness. So if we say that we share in life with God, but we continue living in darkness, we are liars, who

The Helmet of Salvation

don't follow the truth. We should live in the light, where God is. If we live in the light, we have fellowship with each other, and the blood sacrifice of Jesus, God's Son, washes away every sin and makes us clean." 1 John 1:5-7 (ERV)

- **I am fearless, courageous and victorious!** "And do not [for a moment] be frightened *or* intimidated in anything by your opponents *and* adversaries, for such [constancy and fearlessness] will be a clear sign (proof and seal) to them of [their impending] destruction, but [a sure token and evidence] of your deliverance *and* salvation, and that from God." Philippians 1:28 (AMP)

- **I am free!** "Therefore, there is now no condemnation for those who are in Christ Jesus, because through Christ Jesus the law of the Spirit who gives life has set you free from the law of sin and death." Romans 8:1-2

- **I am forgiven!** "...as far as the east is from the west, so far has he removed our transgressions from us." Psalm 103:12

- **I am valuable!** "I praise you because I am fearfully and wonderfully made; your works are wonderful, I know that full well." Psalm 139:14

- **I have hope and a future!** "For I know the thoughts *and* plans that I have for you, says the Lord, thoughts *and* plans for welfare *and* peace and not for evil, to give you hope in your final outcome." Jeremiah 29:11 (AMP)

The helmet covers not only the mind, but also the eyes and ears. Christianity is not merely a religion but a lifestyle. It should govern what we think, how we act, what we allow into our bodies and minds, and what comes out. When we keep our helmets on, this helps to keep the negative out. When we choose to let our guards down and take the helmet off, we are faced with temptation and we give the devil a foothold into areas of our life where he has no business.

I am not saying we are to live holed up in the corner and never set foot out the door. We are free in Christ and free to enjoy this life and all the blessings He has in store for us. We need to be wise in each decision we make. The most important thing we can do on our journey is to set boundaries. We may be surrounded by sin but we don't have to indulge in it.

Decide today what you will allow and won't allow on your radio, television, reading tablet, and in your home. Decide today which relationships are healthy for you and which aren't. Seek God's counsel in this decision and He will guide you. 1 Peter 5:8-9 says, "Be self-controlled and alert. Your enemy the devil prowls around like a roaring lion looking for someone to devour. Resist him, standing firm in the faith, because you know that your brothers throughout the world are undergoing the same kind of sufferings."

Arm Yourself

- "If my house were not right with God, surely he would not have made with me an everlasting covenant, arranged and secured in every part; surely he would not bring to fruition my salvation and grant me my every desire" 2 Samuel 23:5.

- "The Lord is my rock, my fortress and my deliverer; my God is my rock, in whom I take refuge, my shield and the horn of my salvation, my stronghold" Psalm 18:2.

- "Truly my soul finds rest in God; my salvation comes from him" Psalm 62:1.

- "But since we belong to the day, let us be sober, putting on faith and love as a breastplate, and the hope of salvation as a helmet" 1 Thessalonians 5:8.

5

The Shoes of Peace

*"...and with your feet fitted with the readiness
that comes from the gospel of peace."
Ephesians 6: 15*

The shoe is a very appropriate place, I believe, to put our peace. Think about the different types of shoes we wear: tennis shoes for exercise, slippers for lounging, dress shoes for work, and if you are a woman…then you might have several different styles and colors to suite your mood and/or outfit for the day. I think most people don't think about the kind of peace they are going to put on for that day. But let's take a closer look here.

You might wake up to a house full of kids, dishes in the sink and lunches to be made and immediately begin to feel a spirit of dread come knocking on your door. Perhaps you wake up at the crack of dawn to get up and get ready for a job that is filled with hostility, gossip, and backstabbing. Not to mention a boss that seems to be watching you're every move and micromanaging everything you do. When you wake up in the morning and allow that spirit of dread to begin leaking into your mind and heart… your peace goes out the door with it also. You'll find yourself short-tempered with those kids, rushing until your frazzled, and already contemplating the conversations with your boss and

The Shoes of Peace

co-workers that has set you into a bad mood and you haven't even put your slippers on yet. The key here is to set our minds and keep them set...to Peace!

Choose Peace

God's word says, in Romans 12:18, "If it is possible, as long as it depends on you, live at peace with everyone." Note the key phrase here: AS LONG AS IT DEPENDS ON YOU! We don't need to allow our spouse, our children, our friends or circumstances dictate whether or not we have peace. We CHOOSE peace in any and every situation.

Bad health, big decisions, financial pressure, family drama, you name it, there are ample outlets for us to lose our peace. Satan will try to throw into your mind everything that is wrong or could possibly go wrong. God wants you to focus on your blessings, reasons to be grateful and joyful, and all the good things in your life. It is completely up to YOU what you choose to focus on. I realized that the more negative I focused on, the more negative I became. The opposite is also true, the more positive that I focused on, the more positive I became.

When you look back at the pieces of armor we've covered, the helmet of salvation and the belt of truth primarily cover a lot of our minds and thought life. When I think about the shoes of peace and what it protects, I think about our emotions.

We can be guided and even led to make decisions based on our emotions at the time. We can be angry, sad, hurt, happy, excited, overwhelmed, discouraged, insecure, shy, frustrated, cranky, affectionate and frazzled...and all that before noon! Can you imagine living our lives to be guided by how we feel at any given moment? A lot more people live like this than you would imagine!

Forgiveness

If we could stop living based on our emotion or feelings, one improvement might be a lot less divorce. The excuse that people fall out of love with their spouse, in my opinion, is bologna! We need not stay married because of how we feel towards that person on any given day or we are in trouble. There are days I do not like my husband, because of something he said or did that I did not approve of, but do I love him? Yes. Why? Because it is a choice I made at the altar of my church before God and my family that I would love this man for better or worse, richer or poorer, and in sickness and health. Loving someone, just like keeping your peace, is a choice. I choose to love my husband through good times and bad, and annoying times are included. Just as in a marriage, I have heard it said you need to be a professional forgiver; it is the same perspective when keeping your peace.

In Matthew, chapter 18, Peter asks Jesus how often he's expected to forgive those who have done him wrong, seven times? Jesus replies no, try seven times seventy times! In Peter's

The Shoes of Peace

mind, after seven strikes you're out. In Jesus' answer, clearly we are to forgive every time so as not to allow anything to come between Him and us. How does this happen? Well look at what Matthew 6:14-15 says. It explains that when you forgive other people, He will also continue to forgive you. When you stop, so does He. Wow! That is quite a statement. How many people are allowing the roots of unforgiveness to grow bitterness and resentment in their lives? I think both you and me can think of a person or two. What kind of fruit do you think it is producing in their life? What kinds of prayers do you think it is hindering from being answered? Well pretty much all of them.

If He can't forgive you due to some unforgiveness issues between you and another person, that will begin to isolate you from Him and no longer can peace dwell where there is no good soil to sprout. The sooner you deal with the unforgiveness, the sooner He can meet your need. So let's think about this in the perspective of forgiving a prodigal child, an ex-spouse, a mean boss, or a friendship gone sour.

It's not easy but the first step is acknowledging the lingering unforgiveness harbored in your heart and begin laying it at the feet of Jesus. Ask Him to help you forgive. There is nothing wrong in admitting our need for help, especially to the Prince of Peace. He's there to help you forgive. It doesn't punish the other person, but you, to keep an unforgiving attitude in your heart.

The D Word

So what do we need to begin operating in peace? That dreaded D word. That word that is so hard to follow through with. The responsibility we take for our own actions...Discipline.

Nobody really likes that word because it has such a negative connotation to it. We might think of our childhood or even in rearing our own children when we might have been grounded or when daddy went to grab the belt. But, the kind of discipline we are going to talk about is not one we need to fear. It is actually one we should embrace because it comes from our Heavenly Father and he wants nothing more than the absolute very best for our lives. If we will only heed his pruning, pursuing, direction, and yes, even discipline, we will reap a bountiful harvest in our lives. Just look at what Hebrews 12:11 says about it:

"No discipline seems pleasant at the time, but painful. Later on, however it produces a harvest of righteousness and peace for those who have been trained by it."

I went through a period of time where God was disciplining and pruning me in the area of my emotions. One summer, God began to peel the layers back like an onion and revealing the underlying problems under every emotion, feeling, and reaction I was having towards my family. I never realized how much I allowed myself to be controlled by my emotions. I would speak hurtful words and make irrational decisions based on what I felt in the heat of the moment. It constantly threw me into vicious cycles of pathetic attitudes, pity parties and always crying "Why me?" When really it was me that was the problem, not other people. I needed to learn to hold in the reins and taper off the knee-jerk reaction to spit out the first thing that would come to my mind. Whether it be right or wrong, true or not, you were going to hear it!

I began reading an incredible book God laid on my heart by Joyce Meyer, who is one of my favorite Christian authors, called *Living Beyond Your Feelings.* I swear that book was written just for me! The biggest revelation I received when reading that book, that no one ever had told me, was that however I feel when I wake up or in any given moment during the day, I do not have to submit to that feeling or emotion but instead can CHOOSE differently...better.

I say all this to say that before you can ever learn to be at peace with anyone else, you need to learn to be at peace with yourself. I saw what I was doing to myself and to those around me, and I didn't like it. I even got to the point where I did not like me very much. Thank God that He intervened when He did. I began to learn to be at peace with me.

First, He had to undo this tangled mess of emotions that wrapped around me and it was not an overnight thing. Day by day, I received a new revelation, a new word. The more time I spent in His Word, the more it would truly reflect back to me the

Arm Yourself

image of the woman He created me to be. Through that process, He began to take out all the junk: bad attitudes, poor decision making, irrational thinking, overreactions, spiteful words…yea it was ugly.

He began replacing those bad attitudes with joyful attitudes, loving responses, careful decision-making, and wise words of wisdom. My internal dialogue began to change about the world around me, when I began to make an effort to change it about myself. God began with disciplining me from the inside out.

Peace, Be Still

Now we are only human which inherently makes us *not* perfect. So when a challenging person or situation raises its ugly head, we have a choice to make. *Do I respond with peace? Do I respond with sarcasm, hurtful words, or worse?* This is where we not only have the opportunity to choose peace to have a better day, but share peace. People are watching. They know you are a Christian and they are waiting to see if you are going to act like one. We need not leave anyone wondering whether we are or not, based on our reactions to life and other people. We are called to light, so let's shine it on the good and bad.

You could be treated unfairly in the most chaotic of circumstance or even treated badly by people, but choose the higher road, whatever that might be, to keep the peace at all costs. This might mean holding your tongue, thinking of the positive and not the negative, praising someone instead of criticizing them, or whatever God may lay on your heart when handling a difficult situation.

Psalm 34:14 (NLT) says, "Turn away from evil and do good. Search for peace and work to maintain it." What happens when you have been wronged and the other person refuses to reconcile? In this case it is up to you (think back again to Rom. 12:18 "...as far as it depends on you"). You get to decide to let bitterness and unforgiveness eat at you or to forgive them in your heart asking the Lord to heal the wounds and the loss of that relationship.

We can choose to keep our peace or lose our peace. God is calling us to live in peace so we must give it up: give up our need to be right or our need to be heard. If we cannot reconcile that relationship on our own terms, put it in God's hands and in His timing, and let Him work it out His way.

Get Ready

Let's look at Ephesians 6:15 again where it says, "feet fitted with the readiness..." We need to be ready! God's word gets us ready for anything- ready to face our families, our bosses, coworkers, bill collectors, and illness; whatever issue might come our way that day. When we choose to operate in peace we are not showing how calm we can be under pressure but how awesome God is when glorified in us. It truly becomes the peace that transcends all understanding as explained in Philippians 4:7.

When people look at our circumstances and situations, they wonder how we can manage good attitudes and optimism during something so hard and dismal. They will be asking you, "How does she do it?" That is when it opens up the door for us to share His good news: The Gospel of Peace.

Let me just say right here: Don't let someone talk you out of your peace! That is why we don't gossip about others or our husbands. That is why we don't try to gain advice from someone who is not anywhere near qualified to be giving us advice in a particular area. You can choose to keep your peace and you can choose to lose it also. How do we lose it? By giving it away… to another person or situation. No person on this planet or circumstance is worth losing our peace. It is our God given right and fruit of the Spirit. Guard your shoes of peace by tying the laces, strapping the buckle…whatever you need to do to continue treading ahead with readiness to face anything! Isaiah 52: 7 says:

> "How beautiful on the mountains are the feet of those who bring good news, who proclaim peace, who bring good tidings, who proclaim salvation, who say to Zion, "Your God reigns!"

Sharing how we received our peace and learning to maintain our peace is our good news! Share your faith and your testimony! It is our job as Christians to share God's goodness and what He has done for us to inspire others in their own journey and pursuit of God. Showing off your peace shows off on God and His character. He is not a condemning, judging cold and unrelatable God. He is loving and giving and He wants to bless those who love Him and trust Him. "Peacemakers who sow in peace reap a harvest of righteousness" James 3:18.

Arm Yourself

- "You will keep in perfect peace those whose minds are steadfast, because they trust in you" Isaiah 26:3.

- "Though the mountains be shaken and the hills be removed, yet my unfailing love for you will not be shaken nor my covenant of peace be removed," says the Lord, who has compassion on you" Isaiah 54:10.

- "Blessed are the peacemakers, for they will be called children of God" Matthew 5:9.

- "The God of peace will soon crush Satan under your feet" Romans 16:20.

- "Let the peace of Christ rule in your hearts, since as members of one body you were called to peace. And be thankful" Colossians 3:15.

6

The Breastplate of Righteousness

"...and with the breastplate of righteousness in place."
Ephesians 6: 14

When we think about the discipline it takes to begin managing our emotions as we talked about in the last chapter, we begin to see the fruit it produces in our lives. When we are not the center of our own attention, our focus is shifted on where it needs to be. Look at what Hebrews 12:11 says in the Amplified Version:

"For the time being no discipline brings joy, but seems grievous *and* painful; but afterwards it yields a peaceable fruit of righteousness to those who have been trained by it [a harvest of fruit which consists in righteousness—in conformity to God's will in purpose, thought, and action, resulting in right living and right standing with God]."

I believe the very definition of righteousness is laid out in this scripture- "conformity to God's will in purpose, thought and action, resulting in right living and right standing with God." When we invite the Holy Spirit in to do His work, and give permission to God to allow His power to freely be at work in our lives, we can expect results all across the board.

When I asked God to clean out the junk in my emotional life he went a step further, he cleaned out the junk in my financial life too. He put a desire in my heart to better my circumstances, to use wisdom in my money, and gave me a platform to freely discuss finances with my husband.

We went through *Financial Peace University* by Dave Ramsey with our church. We discovered that a lot of the biblical principles laid out for us in God's Word, apply to not just our spiritual, mental, or emotional needs but also to our financial needs. He wanted us to not just trust Him in the mental, but also in the physical. He wanted to show us that He could take our five loaves and two fish, as explained in John 6, and do miracles with it also. We could live debt-free. We could stop being a slave to the lender and begin to bless others financially!

He also began to deal with me in the area of my health. I am not an inherently healthy person and have a prominent distaste for all things green and leafy. Not only was I out of control in just my emotions and behavior, I was out of control in eating habits and exercise habits, or lack thereof.

I lacked discipline all across the board. It didn't just stop for me at one thing, but in many! Think about a person that is driving a car and has no brakes, no steering, and is blindfolded, that was me. Only I didn't see it, I was the one blindfolded. Sooner or later I was going to crash.

God's best for us is not going to involve overly busy schedules that we have no time to breathe, relax, spend time with God, or think about what we eat before we put it in our mouths. It is not going to include keeping up with a lifestyle that we can't afford either. God's best for us will include a balance between work and rest, a healthy mindset and attitude towards life in general, and a desire to be healthy inside and out in every area of our lives.

Choices

Righteousness is having the strength and courage to stand and make the right choices for our families and ourselves. These few examples I have listed are only some of the areas of my life that were not conformed to God's will and purpose. Perhaps healthy habits or your finances are not an area where you need some improvement. It may be something entirely different but I can promise you that when you truly walk with God and allow Him to take the reins of your life as your Heavenly Father, He will begin to point out to you areas you can better yourself. Trust me, it's a lot harder to stay the same than it is to change. I would much rather have God's very best for my life than what I think is best.

The breastplate protects major organs. The heart, lungs, stomach and so on... So let's do what we need to on our part to keep these vital components running efficiently. A Christian woman that is slowed down not by the enemy, but her own poor choices in life, disables herself from tapping into her full God-given potential.

God gave us our bodies as a temple for the Holy Spirit to dwell in. God gave us our money and resources not to squander for our own liking, but to bless others and to use as tools to advance His Kingdom. God gave us media outlets and technology to be informed of affairs of other parts of the world and even situations at our own back door. So what do we do with all of this overwhelming knowledge? We do what we can about it using our time, talents and energy and pray about the rest.

We can't save the world....Jesus already did that. But with what we've been given, let's take care of it, cultivate it and develop it. Everything that God has given us to be the unique individual we are is not a carbon copy of anyone else. We are created to do great Kingdom work! Make the choice today to stop living for yourself and start living for someone else. It starts at home, being missionaries to own children. If we do not talk to them about God and fill their mind with Scripture, the world will be vying for that empty mind space and trying to fill it with all kinds of worldly cares and concerns. He then might ask us to take it one step further and begin to minister to those within our own circle of influence. Those coworkers, waitresses, and neighbors need Jesus too!

Jesus was a perfect example of walking in true righteousness. In the book of Mark it is noted that even the Pharisees said to

Jesus, "...We know that you are a man of integrity. You aren't swayed by others, because you pay no attention to who they are" Mark 12: 14. Let's not be swayed and pressured by others and allow people to tell us how we need to live our lives. Let's stop worrying about being politically correct but biblically accurate! Let's begin making choices that bring us and our families dignity, integrity, uprightness and know we can lay our heads down every night and did the very best we could.

What are you harvesting?

Hebrews 12:11 speaks about a harvest of fruit, I can't help but think about the fruit of the spirit. As you can read in Galatians the fruit of the spirit consists of love, joy, peace, patience, kindness, goodness, faithfulness, and self-control. So when we sow these seeds into our lives a harvest begins to sprout and others can begin to see the results of a life empowered by the Holy Spirit.

Some of the best compliments I have ever gotten is when people comment to me how I may have handled a situation, that I have a caring and compassionate spirit or that they see evidence of a higher power at work within me. Those compliments stop me in my track and remind me that I am not alone.

The Holy Spirit is helping me to harvest these better attributes and more well rounded mindsets that allow me to operate as the woman God created me to be. So when you have someone in your life that is a role model to you, tell him or her how much they mean to you. Tell them what an impact they make on your life. I lost my grandmother a little over a year ago and to this day I stop and think, *Did I really tell her how much I admire and respected her? Did she know what an incredible legacy she left for me?* I am sure that she heard something similar to that once or twice, but hearing encouragement as someone who might be always used to being the encourager feels really good.

Don't be Fooled

When we are trying to do what's right, walk in God's will and let him transform us inside and out, the devil is also waiting and watching. He looks for a weak spot that might make you vulnerable to attacks and fall off the bandwagon.

The devil has no problem letting sinners keep doing their thing, but it is those walking in Christ that he wants to trip up. So be aware, as we have mentioned before, of situations that might give you the opportunity to make a mistake or a bad decision.

We are going to have our slip-ups and that is not anything to beat yourself up over. Ask the Lord to give you wisdom from the situation and discernment to not make the same mistake again.

I remember when my husband and I received the best news! He had just gotten the promotion of a lifetime and we were on track to finally making a much larger dent in our debt. It was reason to celebrate but would you know in that moment I heard, *What makes you think you deserve this?* or *What makes you think you will use this increase in income wisely? Your just going screw this up!* Instead of hanging my head down in defeat and wallowing in those thoughts, I picked myself up and said out loud *I will not screw this up and, devil, I will not listen to you. I will rejoice in the Lord's favor and be faithful and generous just as He is to me!* I had made up my mind and it was done. I will not be fooled into thinking my way out of God's blessing. I will put on my breastplate, with shoulders back, confident of one of my favorite sayings: "The will of God will never take you where the grace of God will not protect you".

By now we have our belt of truth on that is keeping us grounded in God's truth for our lives and our shields of faith oiled with confidence. We have on our helmets of salvation that guards our minds and thoughts from attacks, and the shoes of peace that allow us to share the good news of God's peace in our hearts and lives. Now lets equip ourselves with the breastplate of righteousness and walk in conformity to God's will in our lives with courage and perseverance.

This was the last piece of armor that defends us from the attacks of the enemy and allows no weapon to prevail against us. Next we will talk about our actual weapons that when waged can cause destruction of strongholds and bondage if we learn to yield them daily.

The Breastplate of Righteousness

Arm Yourself

- "Blessed are those who hunger and thirst for righteousness, for they will be filled" Matthew 5:6.

- "For in the gospel the righteousness of God is revealed—a righteousness that is by faith from first to last, just as it is written: "The righteous will live by faith" Romans 1:17.

- "All Scripture is God-breathed and is useful for teaching, rebuking, correcting and training in righteousness…" 2 Timothy 3:16.

7

The Sword of the Spirit

"Take the...sword of the spirit, which is the word of God."
Ephesians 6:17

The sword is our only weapon and the only one we will ever need. It is powerful enough to break generational strongholds, to rip off the chains of oppression, and to slay demons that taunt and torture us with their accusations. Let me remind you that a much greater army stands with us and the Almighty General stands before us ready to help at the request of his name: JESUS! In my mind, I can just imagine how scary it looks to the demons from hell when a daughter of the King stands with her armor on and a sword ready to strike. Let us dive into how to use this magnificent piece of weaponry!

So what is this weapon? The bible states it is the Word of God. There are two parts to this weapon of ours. The first is in how we apply God's word to our lives. The second is in speaking the Word of God over our lives which in turn releases the power of the Holy Spirit to work on our behalf. So get ready to hear some of God's word heavily in this chapter, as it is only fitting that we take a serious look at our sword.

In Hebrews 9:6-10, it explains the old order of things and religious practice when the priest was the only one allowed to enter the inner room, only once a year, and always with a blood sacrifice with which to atone for his sins and the peoples. Let's look at what verse 9 and 10 say:

> "This is an illustration for the present time, indicating that the gifts and sacrifices being offered were not able to clear the conscience of the worshiper. They are only a matter of food and drink and various ceremonial washings- external regulations applying until the time of the new order."

Now let's cross reference what Romans 14:17 says in the New Living Translation, "For the kingdom of God is not a matter of what we eat or drink, but of goodness and peace and joy in the Holy Spirit." The new order began when Jesus Christ became the ultimate sacrifice for us, tore the veil, and allowed us to come into the inner room, straight to the very throne room of God to fellowship with Him. He no longer wanted it to be a matter of religious practice and regulation. He wanted us to form a true relationship with Him by breaking down these barriers. Let's look back again at Hebrews in chapter 10, verses 15-18 that says:

> "The Holy Spirit also testifies to us about this. First he says: "This is the covenant I will make with them after that time, says the Lord. I will put my laws in their hearts, and I will write them on their minds." Then he adds:

Arm Yourself

"Their sins and lawless acts I will remember no more. And where these have been forgiven, sacrifice for sin is no longer necessary."

Even the Holy Spirit himself testifies that the laws He will write on our hearts and minds come from Him! So what exactly is he writing? God's word! When we get to the point that God's Word becomes so engrained in our thoughts...we change from the inside out. We become stronger. We become wiser and more adapt at handling life's challenges.

Our Sword: Part One

Now let's look at the first part of our sword which is reading God's word and understanding how we need to apply it to our lives. Think about it this way, when you sign up to take a physics class, but you never bother to buy the book, will you pass once the exam comes? When you go in to sit at a book club and are asked a challenging question about something that happens in the chapter but you never read the book, will you be ready to answer? The same logic applies here. When we become a Christian and are determined to live for God, does that just come from good works and ourselves? No! We need to open the bible and read it, DAILY, not just on Sunday mornings or at bible study.

Everyday we are faced with new challenges and some may seem insurmountable. Some may even completely catch us off guard. But, thank goodness, the Lord's mercy is fresh every day and His grace is always there for us. If we would only tap into it, a new word exactly for the season we are in, is in there waiting for us to read and soak up. All God asks us to do is open the book and study it so that when a test comes we will pass with flying colors.

Let's look at Luke, chapter eight about the parable of the sower. A Farmer sows seed on four different types of ground: some of it the birds ate it up, some fell on rock where there was no moisture and it withered, some fell on the thorns and it choked the plants and some fell on good soil and it yielded a bountiful crop. Let's look at how Jesus explains the meaning of all four:

"This is the meaning of the parable: The seed is the Word of God. Those along the path are the ones who hear, and then the devil comes and takes away the word from their hearts, so that they may not believe and be saved. Those on the rocky ground are the ones who receive the word with joy when they hear it, but they have no root. They believe for a little while, but in the time of testing they fall away. The seed that fell among the thorns stands for those who hear, but as they go on their way they are choked by life's worries, riches and pleasures and they do not mature. But the seed on good soil stands for those with a noble and good heart, who hear the word, retain it, and by persevering produce a crop." Luke 8:11-15

Which Soil are You?

There are four different types of soil at work here, let's get a closer look into each one. I have given each soil a different name to better relate to us in our walk with God. There is the "Victim Soil" which is the birds, the "Socialite Soil" which is the rocky soil, the "Baby Soil" which is the thorns, and the "Mature Soil" which is the good soil.

The "Victim Soil" are those that blame all their problems on other people and think its everyone else's fault. They are the way they are because of their circumstances and they are never going to change. These people might be stubborn and have a sense of helplessness and hopelessness. They might even be prone to depression and suck the life right out of other people. It may even be physically, mentally, and emotionally draining to be around these kinds of people. They have a sense of entitlement and when things do not go as planned, they let everyone around them know about it and do not even stop to count their blessings. Perhaps, they go and hear the message at church every Sunday and never let it penetrate to their hearts and minds to promote real change. This may seem a bit harsh, but I am willing to bet, we all know someone like this.

The "Socialite Soil" is someone who hears the message of good news but because they neglect to provide that rich moisture from daily soaking in God's word they let it die mostly by being too busy or when hard times and trials come their way. They are

The Sword of the Spirit

consumed with filling their calendars with church activities and events that might make them feel better about themselves, but they neglect to remember what it is all about. They volunteer for the homeless ministry not to be a blessing to others and make a difference, but instead to have something else to put on their volunteer resume. Perhaps they look at church as a gathering of friends rather than a place of hope for the hurting and encouragement in their own personal walk.

The "Baby Soil" never matures. They are like the wandering Israelite who continues to whine and complain forgetting all the marvelous deeds God has already done for them and never taking their relationship with God to the next level. They never seem to get past their original level of faith from when they first got saved. You might even go so far as to say they believe in God and claim themselves to be a Christian, but it doesn't go much further than that. They believe they are here to sleep, eat, play, and die and they will get to the matters of making right with their Maker when they get to meet Him. Matthew 7:21 and 23 in the NIV, clearly explains what Jesus thinks about these:

> "Not everyone who says, 'Lord, Lord,' will enter the kingdom of heaven, but only the one who does the will of my Father who is in Heaven...Then I will tell them plainly, 'I never knew you. Away from me you evildoers!'

The last soil is the "Mature Soil". These people not only hear God's word but act on what they hear. They stand up for change, soak in God's word, and let it marinate in their hearts and souls until it produces a real and lasting change in their hearts that begins to overflow into all areas of their life. This is where we should aspire to be if we are not already there.

Don't be discouraged! If you find yourself to fit into one of these categories or a combination of a couple of them, you can cultivate that soil until it becomes mature. The fact you are reading this far into the book means you are not too far-gone! No one is too far-gone for the Lord to renew and restore and put back on track.

In Hebrews 4:12 it states, "...the word of God is alive and active. Sharper than any double-edged sword, it penetrates even to dividing soul and spirit, joints and marrow; it judges the thoughts and attitudes of the heart." The first part says God's Word is living and active. When you read God's Word, it says something completely different to you than anyone else. It is alive and the vessel most used by God to speak into our hearts and lives about our current needs. It will pierce our hearts with words of wisdom that reach into the deepest, darkest, most hidden parts of ourselves that we may not have even known about. God's word gives us wisdom in our situation, discernment in decisions, hope when we are lost and encouragement for the every day.

Our Sword: Part Two

Speaking the word of God over our lives is powerful and in turn releases the Holy Spirit to go to work in our lives. When we speak the promises of life into our dead situations, we begin setting things into motion that will in turn yield a harvest of blessings. Let's look at a few of these examples of what I mean by speaking God's word into your life:

> "Truly I tell you, if you have faith as small as a mustard seed, you can say to this mountain, 'Move from here to there,' and it will move. Nothing will be impossible for you" Matt 17:20.

This scripture speaks courage into our situations that might be riddled with fear, trepidation and anxiety about the future or outcome of something going on in our lives. One of my favorite Joyce Meyer quotes is "Do it afraid!" When a task seems daunting to us, we would rather just retreat back into our comfort zones. But scripture states that with God on our side we have nothing to fear!

> "When I called you, you answered me, you made me bold and stouthearted" Psalm 138: 3.

We can know that when we call upon the Lord He hears us and will answer us. Our prayers never fall on deaf ears. Although our answer or breakthrough or healing may seem slow in coming, it will come in God's way and God's timing. Until then we need to walk in confidence knowing God has got this and ask Him to make us bold to face the situation even when we don't yet see the end result. Our faith will be a lot less likely to waver as we learn to practice it with bold confidence!

> "Though hostile nations surrounded me, I destroyed them all with the authority of the Lord. Yes, they surrounded and attacked me, but I destroyed them all with the authority of the Lord" Psalm 118:10-11

Just hearing this scripture should make chill bumps all over our arms! We have authority over the dominion of darkness! We can command the devil to leave our homes, our families, and our minds and he has to leave!

> "Everyone who calls on the name of the Lord will be saved" Romans 10:13.

No matter where we have been, no matter our past or family heritage, no matter our sin or our current situation, we can all become the person God created us to be. God promises that all we have to do is call upon His name and we will be saved, restored, renewed, healed, loved, and anchored into Him! We just have to make that first step and realize that without Him we are nothing and can do nothing; at least nothing of any true and lasting value.

The Sword of the Spirit

Nothing worth having ever comes easy. It comes by hard work, and let me assure you this is hard work. It doesn't come easy nor does it come naturally. It's just like when I first went to the gym and had my first session with a personal trainer. She had me doing all kinds of strength training and cardio exercises and stretched me to limits that I didn't know my body could go. Afterwards, I was so incredibly sore that Ibuprofen and Epsom Salt baths were barely making a dent in my pain levels. But that pain was my muscles tearing, growing, and strengthening so that the next time I worked out, it wasn't going to hurt as bad.

If you don't use your muscles, you lose them. But when they are stretched and grown during times of hard exercise, they will be able to hold more and lift higher. It's the same thing with your spiritual arm muscle that waves your sword. It may feel awkward putting scripture all over your house, your car, your desktop, or wherever, but the more you commit these scriptures to memory the more you will see results happening all around you-in your personal, work, or home life.

It is a gradual change, not something that happens overnight. When you wake up in the morning, I encourage you to start reading God's word aloud. Find a scripture that speaks life to you for that day and meditate on it. Say it, speak it; yell it if you have to! Write it on a chalkboard and discuss it with your family. One of my favorite things to do is read it in several different bible translations until it pierces my heart with it's truth. Bottom line here is get some WORD into your heart, life, family, finances, etc.. and see if things don't begin to change… for the better!

Speaking God's word and claiming scriptures over our situation doesn't have to be just speaking. It can be singing, worshipping, praising, and shouting. You don't need to have the best voice but a heart full of sincere praise to God. It sets your mind free and gets the devil to flee!

When we looked at the shield of faith, we talked about faith stealers and faith builders and reading God's word was one of the faith builders. With the belt of truth we began replacing Satan's lies with truth from God's Word. With the helmet of salvation we talked about defining our personal identity and kingdom identity and the kingdom identity is found clearly laid out in His word stating who we are and what God expects from us. With the shoes of peace all we have to do is what is said in Phillipians 4:9: "Whatever you have learned or received or heard from me, or seen in me—put it into practice. And the God of peace will be with you." With our breastplate in place, we can stand firm on God's promises that he has given us through the hope given by His Holy Spirit. The recurrent theme here is God's word, without it we are only able to defend because all we would have is our armor. With our swords we can begin taking ground and advancing against Satan.

Arm Yourself

- "As the rain and the snow come down from heaven, and do not return to it without watering the earth and making it bud and flourish, so that it yields seed for the sower and bread for the eater, so is my word that goes out from my mouth: It will not return to me empty, but will accomplish what I desire and achieve the purpose for which I sent it" Isaiah 55:10-11.

- "I have hidden your word in my heart that I might not sin against you" Psalm 119:11.

- "For everything that was written in the past was written to teach us, so that through the endurance taught in the Scriptures and the encouragement they provide we might have hope" Romans 15:4.

8

The Robe of Love

"...And over all these virtues put on love, which binds them all together in perfect unity."
Colossians 3:14

The robe of love is not something you will find in the Bible. It is not the 7th piece of armor as listed in Ephesians. So please do not drive yourself crazy looking in your concordance and footnotes for something called "The Robe of Love". This is purely something that was birthed within me as I was studying the different pieces of armor.

If you look at pictures of Roman soldiers they have all of these pieces of armor that we have already described and you will also see a robe, usually red, underneath the armor. In Colossians, we are asked to clothe ourselves with love, so I definitely think it is safe to say that the red robe can symbolize the robe of love that we are asked to clothe ourselves with in Colossians.

Although this is written last, this is actually the first thing that needs to go on before any other piece of our armor. This robe was put on underneath the armor to keep these very large and heavy pieces of armor from chafing the soldiers. So without putting love on first, what testimony, what impact, what kind of unity, as explained in the above scripture, will we have? Without it, it is all in vain, and it just won't work. How, you might ask? Let's see what 1 Corinthians 13 has to say in the Message Version:

"If I speak with human eloquence and angelic ecstasy but don't love, I'm nothing but the creaking of a rusty gate. If I speak God's Word with power, revealing all his mysteries and making everything plain as day, and if I have faith that says to a mountain, "Jump," and it jumps, but I don't love, I'm nothing. If I give everything I own to the poor and even go to the stake to be burned as a martyr, but I don't love, I've gotten nowhere. So, no matter what I say, what I believe, and what I do, I'm bankrupt without love. Love never gives up…Love never dies. Inspired speech will be over some day; praying in tongues will end; understanding will reach its limit. We know only a portion of the truth, and what we say about God is always incomplete. But when the Complete arrives, our incompletes will be canceled… But for right now, until that completeness, we have three things to do to lead us toward that consummation: Trust steadily in God, hope unswervingly, love extravagantly. And the best of the three is love." 1 Corinthians 13

I believe there are three areas of love we need to take a closer look at. Learning to love God, love ourselves, and love others.

Love God

Let's first look at what the bible says about loving God. In 1 John 5:3, he says, "Loving God means obeying his commands. And God's commands are not too hard for us..." When you first read this you might think, *Ok I just need to follow the Ten Commandments and I am good.* God has certain things laid out in His word for us to follow and accomplish, of course. He has role models to live by which is also good. But, neither good works nor following the Ten Commandments is going to get us in good with our Heavenly Father. He wants us to do what *He* says. Those things listed like in Philippians, that we have heard and seen in Him, He wants us to put *that* into practice. He wants to see our faith in action. He wants to see us overcome our tests and turn them into testimonies. He wants us to share the good news with others, and spend time with Him every day. He wants us to use the gifts and talents he bestowed on us to His glory.

Why do I write to tell you all of this in the first place? Because, I love my God! I love a God who has saved me from a path of destruction. I love a God who has poured out His blessings upon me when I felt the least worthy. I love Him, because He loved me first-even when he didn't have to. God is constantly doing things for us, openly and behind the scenes.

Even when a prayer has taken ten years to reap any obvious answer or produce any fruit, it doesn't mean God wasn't working in that situation. He works on His own time in His own way. If we can wait patiently and love Him through the difficult situation, we are so much more grateful when our breakthrough comes. He is also more likely to bless us and care about those little things that we care about when we offer up to him an attitude of thankfulness and gratitude.

Think about a parent who might have an extremely difficult and whiny child. Do you think that parent wants to bless that child with good gifts or grant their every request? No. But even when we are acting whiny and being difficult, God still wants to bless us, love us, and bestow good gifts to His children.

I used to help a good friend of mine film weddings on the weekends. These lavish events are held at some of the most ornate and beautiful churches or posh venues in Dallas, Texas. It is always quite the experience to be at one of these weddings. During one of the ceremonies, as I was manning the balcony camera, the pastor speaking at the wedding said something that stuck with me. He said "God is the kind of person that even when you kick him in the shin...He's worried about whether or not *you* hurt your foot."

God loves us even when we are unlovable. That makes me love Him more! Despite my flaws, imperfections and numerous inadequacies, he never gives up on me. He wants nothing but the best for me. Sometimes that means answering my prayers and sometimes that means staying silent for a period of time.

Sometimes what I pray for is not what I need, and it is hard to take that in also.

Since God is referred to as our Heavenly Father, a little discipline is not far off, as is with an earthly father. He disciplines us because He loves us, He blesses us because He loves us, He holds our hand through the storm because He loves us, and He shines the light in our darkness because He loves us. All he wants in return is our love and complete and utter devotion to Him. All He wants is our fellowship. We were created for Him…to worship Him!

When we are not spending time with Him or sitting at the feet of Jesus, whether that might be in the car on the way to work, or on a lunch break, or early in the morning before anyone wakes up, or in the quiet of your bedroom after everyone is asleep, then we are missing something. We have a void in our hearts and in our lives that only He can fill. When we pursue relationships, children, material possessions, social status or job titles to try to fill that void, we fall short. As a matter of fact, everything falls short! Nothing can compare to what fills us in the presence of the Lord. After we have had that quiet time with Him, it shows to everyone around us too. When we take that time to dive into what God's love truly is and how all encompassing it is, we can't help but return that love to Him and allow it to pour out into those around us. Just look at what Psalm 90:14 says, "Satisfy us in the morning with your unfailing love, that we may sing for joy and be glad all of our days."

The Robe of Love

As of this writing, I am currently going through the "Breaking Free" bible study by Beth Moore, which I highly recommend. I am on the chapter, "God's unfailing love" and how appropriate that I would study it as I write this chapter. It goes into great depth and detail using profound commentary and scripture with God's love as its foundation. I felt like I was washed in a bath of God's love when I was reading, dissecting and soaking in this bible study.

For some of you, you might think feeling this kind of love is beyond you or impossible. You might even wish that you loved God more than you do now. Don't despair! Bring those requests to the Almighty's throne and ask Him for more love or for you to love Him more. He will graciously grant this request, I promise! Why? Because I am convinced that "...neither death nor life, neither angels nor demons, neither the present nor the future, nor any powers, neither height nor depth, nor anything else in all creation, will be able to separate us from the love of God that is in Christ Jesus our Lord" Romans 8: 38-39.

Beth Moore says, "If you can't think of a time when you felt lavished in God's love, ask Him to make you more aware. God's love is demonstrative. Ask Him to widen your spiritual vision so that you can behold unexpected evidences of God's amazing love" (1).

Love Yourself

This topic might seem a little taboo to your average Christian. We are taught to put others first, and pride and vanity are looked down upon. With the unrealistic pictures of women and men on magazine covers and airbrushed and edited photos everywhere, it's easy to see how insecurity has become more of an epidemic than an isolated problem for few people.

But we must first learn to love ourselves before we can properly love others. God even says it in His word! In Mark 12:30-31, He at first commands us to love Him with all of our hearts, minds and strength. He then asks us to love our neighbor as we love ourselves. If we don't first love ourselves, what makes us think we can even begin to show love to others?

This is an area where I have struggled immensely. I have come from a point of hating myself, second-guessing every decision I have ever made, mountains of insecurity, and feelings of unworthiness. I even went to the extreme of just wanting my life to be over, thinking it would make *other* people's lives better. But, boy was I mistaken! Satan wanted to take me out with my self-condemning thoughts so I would not be a threat to him!

Listen, believer, when you are a Bible quoting, Holy Spirit operating, daughter of the King, you are a force to be reckoned with! If Satan can pull the wool over your eyes and make you think life isn't worth living, then He will! If he has used this tactic

The Robe of Love

on you in the past, he will use it again. Insecurity is a demon I have to conquer over and over again. With God's help, I know I can. So let the negative thoughts, and hateful internal dialogue stop...TODAY. Yes, today you can make a decision to stop. It won't be an overnight thing, but it is a process and boy does God love processes. As messed up as the process was that got me to the self-hatred pity party I threw in my mind, I knew it would take a miracle to reprogram my mind and to begin thinking positively about my future and myself. Thanks to Jesus, He is a miracle worker!

Ladies, we have got to stop beating ourselves up when things don't always go our way. We need to let go of these fairytale expectations that no one will ever live up to and cut our husbands and our kids some slack. We humans, as a whole, are not perfect, never have been and never will be.

So let's stop trying to run a perfect household with the dishes being washed every night and the laundry being taken care of at all times and dinner being on the table by 5pm. Now we can strive to keep and maintain an orderly home because we don't want to live in chaos. But for most wives, mothers, and women I know most of this is not done everyday.

Let's stop wasting time and money trying to keep up with the joneses and start being content. Hmmm...let's think about this for a moment. Contentment...let that word just sink in. You don't have to be happy with your circumstances but you do need to learn to be content with them. A great quote I love to hear from Joyce Meyer is "Enjoy where you are on the way to where you are going." So if you don't quite have that big house yet, or that new car, or that promotion at work...whatever it may be, pray about it and see if God wants you to even have that thing in the first place. He knows what is good for you and if you will even be grateful for it after you get it.

Let's take it to an even deeper level. You may not have that strong marriage you were hoping for but keep praying for that spouse and do your part on the Holy Spirit's behalf to foster an environment of healing, restoration, and growth in that relationship. You might have some really deep wounds from a past hurt that are at times too painful to look at which then creates unresolved issues that spill over into other parts of your life, but don't give up. God sees the deepest, darkest parts of your heart that you have locked up and thrown away the key. Jesus has the key that will unlock it and after peeling back some of this hurt, he will reveal a treasure worth more than any amount of gold. You just may be sick and tired of your situation; perhaps you are fed up and overwhelmed. God sees that too and he catches every teardrop. He is holding out His arms asking to jump in and help you. Life is messy and chaotic and people get hurt along the way, but we were never meant to do it alone. All He asks us to do is trust Him and love Him.

So with this confidence and while we may still be in the middle of our mess, give yourself permission to make mistakes, fall down, and have a bad day. Don't be so hard on yourself and stop comparing yourself with other people. Do not envy someone else's walk with the Lord. You don't know what it took to get her there and if you knew all the details you probably wouldn't ever pray for that. Bottom line is we all have our stories, our past, and our testimonies that got us where we are today.

Love yourself in the middle of it! God loves you! He loves every fiber and stitch of heartaches, failures, and faults that are also interwoven with strengths, victories, and beauty that when he steps back and sees the big picture is a masterpiece that can't compare with anyone or anything else.

Grab your Bible and write down some of the love scriptures at the end of this chapter, and read them aloud to yourself. Put them on your bathroom mirror, in the car, or in your purse. Do whatever it takes to begin loving yourself the way you should. This kind of love is not vain or prideful, but full of selflessness and compassion. When you can give yourself a break from blasting yourself all day with negativity and "I should have handled this better mindset", pick yourself up and keep moving forward.

"I'm not saying that I have this all together, that I have it made. But I am well on my way, reaching out for Christ, who has so wondrously reached out for me. Friends, don't get me wrong: By no means do I count myself an expert in all of this, but I've got my eye on the goal, where God is beckoning us onward—to Jesus. I'm off and running, and I'm not turning back" Philippians 3:14 (MSG).

Love others

When we truly learn how to love God and ourselves...the rest will flow into the others. Look at what 1 John 4:7-8, 19-20 says:

Dear friends, let us love one another, for love comes from God. Everyone who loves has been born of God and knows God. Whoever does not love does not know God, because God is love... We love because he first loved us. Whoever claims to love God yet hates a brother or sister is a liar. For whoever does not love their brother or sister, whom they have seen, cannot love God, whom they have not seen."

We are commanded to love our brothers and sisters. That does not just mean our own flesh and blood but all of those around us, the ones easy to love and the ones not so easy to love. The ex husband, the prodigal son, the difficult mother in law, the overbearing boss, the snobby acquaintance at church. You know whom I am talking about; I think a few faces flashed before your eyes too.

I also understand that there are some extreme circumstances where perhaps some mental and physical abuse was involved and that makes things much more complicated, but not impossible. I am not saying we need to necessarily buddy up with these people

The Robe of Love

and go out of our way to see them. But we need to love them to Jesus. Even if that is from afar, there is no greater spiritual warfare being fought than if someone that has hurt you has crossed your mind and instead of ripping them apart mentally, you drop to your knees and pray for them and the salvation of their souls.

Have you heard the famous quote people say, "Hurting people hurt people"? It is true. Most people that hurt others are physically and verbally abusive, because that's all they know or that's how they grew up. Does it excuse their actions? No. But it does create a stronghold in their life that Jesus wants broken over them just as much as He wants yours to be broken. You are not more favored sitting in the suburbs than a woman sitting in prison. 2 Peter 3:9 says, "...The Lord isn't slow about keeping his promises, as some people think he is. In fact, God is patient, because he wants everyone to turn from sin and no one to be lost." We are *ALL* God's children and when you hurt, he hurts.

This is where a key component comes in when it comes to loving others...forgiveness. We touched on this a bit when we were talking about our shoes of peace, but let's go a bit deeper here. You may need to even forgive yourself for something you have done to someone else or you might need to forgive them.

For some, this might be difficult. The other person may have already passed away, be in prison, or you just may not have any contact with them. If that is the case, stop whatever you are doing and drop to your knees and ask the Lord to help you forgive them. I stress this point to be very important because God stresses this to be so important in His word. Let's look at what the Bible says about forgiveness:

> "For if you forgive other people when they sin against you, your heavenly Father will also forgive you. But if you do not forgive others their sins, your Father will not forgive your sins" Matthew 6:14-15.

Nobody's sins are worse than others; He views it all the same. No sin is too big for God to forgive and so it is definitely not too big for you to forgive either. Here is the cool part, once a sin is forgiven, its not just forgiven it is forgotten! "I, even I, am He Who blots out *and* cancels your transgressions, for My own sake, and I will not remember your sins" Isaiah 43:25-26 (MSG).

This point is imperative for us to embrace. When we forgive someone, we need to move on. Don't carry it into the next relationship; don't harbor bitterness and resentment anymore. Don't make your current family or friends pay for the sins of someone in the past. Let's remember what our definition of love is in 1 Corinthians 13:5 says, "Love… does not dishonor others, it is not self-seeking, it is not easily angered, it keeps no record of wrongs." If God is not going to keep a record of our wrongs then what gives us a right to?

This is critical for us to grasp! Until we learn to forgive others, our walk with God is hindered. So let's break down any barriers that keep us from loving others to the full extent and receiving God's love in abundance. Let's also ask God to help us forgive others so He can fully forgive our shortcomings as well.

Love = Joy

Did you know that joy equals love? We can't have one without the other. Let's see how:

"As the Father has loved me, so have I loved you. Now remain in my love. If you keep my commands, you will remain in my love, just as I have kept my Father's commands and remain in his love. I have told you this so that my joy may be in you and that your joy may be complete. My command is this: Love each other as I have loved you" John 15: 9-12.

When we stay within the commands of love as God has so eloquently displayed in the Bible that tells us how we are to love Him and how much He loves us, that is how we "remain in his love". He then goes on to say that when this happens He puts His joy in us so that our joy may be complete.

When we can learn to properly love God, love ourselves and love others, we are bound to experience the fullness of God's joy in our lives! What kind of joy are we talking about though?

Let's look at what Nehemiah 8:10 says, "...For the joy of the Lord is your strength". This joy comes when we let God's love pour out into us and into others. We can't help but share God's love and the joy it brings when it also brings us strength through the everyday trials and the catastrophic life events. We need God's strength, and that comes from a supernatural joy deep down inside which allows us to love God even in the middle of the storm.

Let's look back at our verse at the beginning of this chapter, "...And over all these virtues put on love, which binds them all together in perfect unity", Colossians 3:14. I think you can see now why love is the robe we put on underneath our armor. Love is binding! It binds us together with Him and to each other; it is the underlying glue that holds the armor together.

Arm Yourself

- "Above all, love each other deeply, because love covers over a multitude of sins" 1 Peter 4:8.

- "Because he loves me," says the Lord, "I will rescue him; I will protect him, for he acknowledges my name. He will call on me, and I will answer him; I will be with him in trouble, I will deliver him and honor him. With long life I will satisfy him and show him my salvation" Psalm 91:14-16.

- "There is no fear in love. But perfect love drives out fear, because fear has to do with punishment. The one who fears is not made perfect in love" 1 John 4:18.

- "Yes, God loved the world so much that he gave his only Son, so that everyone who believes in him would not be lost but have eternal life" John 3:16.

9

The Power of Prayer

"...And pray in the Spirit on all occasions with all kinds of prayers and requests. With this in mind, be alert and always keep on praying for all the Lord's people. Pray also for me, that whenever I speak, words may be given me so that I will fearlessly make known the mystery of the gospel, for which I am an ambassador in chains. Pray that I may declare it fearlessly, as I should."
Ephesians 6:18-20

The scripture above finishes out Ephesians 6, so it is only fitting that it finishes out our book as well. Prayer is our communication vehicle to God. It doesn't need to be some eloquent speech. It should come easy and it needs to be like we are talking to a friend. God wants us to be candid, frank, honest, and boldly and confidently approach the throne room with all of our prayer requests as Paul tells us too.

Psalms is full of heart wrenching raw emotion from King David. God heard him and honored him for his honesty. He loved David and He loves you and me too. He wants us to bring all of our worries, concerns, fears, and praises to Him. Philippians 4:6 says to bring every situation to God. He also mentions to do it with thanksgiving! We don't make our list of demands and say

"God this is what I need you to fix, oh, and can you do it by Friday, because that works best for me." No, no, no! God knows what you need and what is good for you. His timing is perfect and knows what we need just when we need it. Sometimes the answer is yes, no or wait and we need to learn to be ok with that.

Quiet Time

Prayer is not a one-way street; it is not just a time for us to talk and Him to hear. We need to take the time to sit and "Be still and know that He is God" as Psalm 46:10 says. Sometimes it helps to just be quiet and play some worship music and see what God puts in your heart. Sometimes the words of a worship song seem to come alive and speak right into the core of your being, confirming a word from the Lord. He might bring a scripture to mind that requires further study.

Sometimes He just wants to revel in you spending time with Him. This is what some people might refer to as quiet time. Setting aside a time everyday to pray, worship, and soak in His presence. In that very moment He refreshes me and reminds me of the bigger picture. It helps me keep my mind off of myself and reminds me "this too shall pass". It keeps my flesh in check and sometimes I need that! Sometimes I need to be reminded that I am not the center of my own universe, nor my husband's, or my kids...but He is!

Arm Yourself

Prayer = Power

James 5:16 says, "The prayers of a righteous man are powerful and effective". Wow! That pumps me up just reading that! A prayerful life is a powerful life! The Lord is tired of only being remembered at Christmas, Easter, and when you need something.

Think about if your child only called you twice a year and when they ran out of money! That would get really old after a while and you might even dread answering the phone when their name popped up on your caller ID. Well imagine if that son or daughter was one that came to drop you off and pick you up from your root canal, called just to say hello and tell you they love you, and spent quality time with you as often as he/she could. Your relationship would be stronger, because the more time invested in the relationship the closer you two would become.

It's not any different with Jesus! Spend more time with Him, loving on Him, talking with Him, worshipping Him, and just inviting Him to join you in your day's activities. Your prayers will naturally become more in tune to His will and His vision for you. You'll find your will and His begin to mesh together. You will begin to want for your life what God wants for your life.

We've already talked about the power of speaking God's word into our lives in the Sword of the Spirit chapter. So when we pray we are also continually driving a wedge between Satan and his plans for us as we loosen the Holy Spirit to be at work in our lives.

Praying for Others

Paul reminds us in our bible verse to pray for all of the Lord's people. When we pray we don't need to be selfish and only involve our prayers around our immediate family's needs and ourselves. We need to also remember to pray for others, not just say we are going to.

Something I notice people say on Facebook when someone posts a trial they may be going through is "I will pray for you". I have always wondered though, *how many people actually do pray for that person,* or has it become an automatic response nowadays like when someone says "Bless you" when they sneeze? I have made a mental note to myself that when scrolling through my newsfeed to stop and pray for them before I look at anything else and truly intercede on that person's behalf.

When I am face to face with someone, if the situation will allow or the person, I ask him or her to hold my hand and pray about the situation right then. I don't want to be all "talk". I want other people to see my faith in action. Not to give myself the glory but know I mean what I say when I say that prayer is important.

I received a phone call today letting me know that a family with four children had their house burned down a couple of days ago. This family needs a miracle. They have to start over completely! Now there are insurance companies and family members and charitable organizations that can step in and help in times like these, but when you might have no money or items to donate it doesn't mean you do nothing! None of the kids are in the same size as my kids as far as clothes go and I may not have very much money but I can offer up prayers. God says MY prayers and YOURS too, are powerful and effective! In situations like these, prayers can help put things in motion when they are specific like praying for swift remediation from the insurance company and perhaps an overflow of comfort and peace during the overwhelming grief and loss over their family home.

Prayers of Many

Our prayers do not fall on deaf ears. In fact, Matthew 18:20 says when two or more come together in prayer, God is right there with them! Look at what the Message version says: "... When two of you get together on anything at all on earth and make a prayer of it, my Father in heaven goes into action..." I love this translation! Jesus says His Father goes into action! I love knowing that God is actively participating, moving, and shifting things in my life and answering my prayers...even when I don't feel it!

When my husband and I are desperately seeking God's will for a big decision we need to make or a healing that needs to happen, we stop what we are doing, hold hands, and pray together over the situation. Every time we pray, I imagine Jesus standing right there next to us with His hands on our shoulders, like a Pastor would, praying right alongside us to His Father. In Ecclesiastes 4:12 it says, "Though one may be overpowered, two can defend themselves. A cord of three strands is not quickly broken." When we join together as a body of believers or a family of believers we become a force so powerful against evil spirits at work in our lives, that demons tremble! Your prayers make hell shake! Satan will do everything he can to make you think prayer doesn't work and God isn't there, but don't you dare listen! I can't tell you how many times I have had people call me and say "Were you praying for me? Because I could feel it! Thank you for your prayers!" Even Paul shares something similar in 2 Corinthians 1:8-11:

> "We do not want you to be uninformed, brothers and sisters, about the troubles we experienced in the province of Asia. We were under great pressure, far beyond our ability to endure, so that we despaired of life itself. Indeed, we felt we had received the sentence of death. But this happened that we might not rely on ourselves but on God, who raises the dead. He has delivered us from such a deadly peril, and he will deliver us again. On him we have set our hope that he will continue to deliver us, as you help us by your prayers. Then many will give thanks on our behalf for the gracious favor granted us in answer to the prayers of many."

Paul even acknowledges that the "prayers of many" helped him endure despair that was "far beyond his ability to endure". So my friends if it was beyond his natural ability that means he had *supernatural* ability that helped him rise up from the dead and persevere! Our prayers have that same power! All we have to do is release it through prayer!

I encourage you, my sister in Christ, that the power displayed in the Bible did not die with Jesus on the cross. It lives inside of you! We might be discouraged at times that make us feel like we are the only few that still live for Jesus and uphold the values, principles, and commands in the Bible but don't let that discourage you from walking out your faith anyway! We are not alone! We are not even outnumbered! There is an army of angels walking behind every believer.

The world was wicked when Noah built his ark, but rather than destroying the whole world and starting from scratch, God spared Noah's life and his family! Even when Sodom and Gomorrah was spewing with evil, Abraham prayed on Lot's behalf and asked the Lord to spare his family from certain destruction. God hears our prayers, sees our effort, and knows our inmost parts and deepest and darkest fears. He knows our past and our victories; He knows our strengths and our potential also. I love what it says in 2 Chronicles 16:9, "For the eyes of the Lord range throughout the earth to strengthen those whose hearts are fully committed to him."

The Power of Prayer

I pray this book encourages you in your walk to know that nothing you have gone through or are about to go through is a surprise to Him. I pray this book helps you to arm yourself with the truth and power that we as Christians have and the knowledge on how to wield the armor and weapons that have divine power to demolish strongholds.

Arm Yourself

- "The Lord is near to all who call on him, to all who call on him in truth" Psalm 145:18.

- "The Lord is far from the wicked, but he hears the prayer of the righteous" Proverbs 15:29.

- "Pray diligently. Stay alert, with your eyes wide open in gratitude. Don't forget to pray for us, that God will open doors for telling the mystery of Christ...Pray that every time I open my mouth I'll be able to make Christ plain as day to them" Colossians 4:2.

"Finally, be strong in the Lord and in his mighty power. Put on the full armor of God, so that you can take your stand against the devil's schemes."
Ephesians 6: 10-11

A Prayer to Arm Yourself

"Heavenly Father I pray that you would help me to clothe myself with the robe of love that binds my armor together perfectly. Jesus I ask that you would help me to walk in God's love and allow it to pour out of me into others today.

Help me Lord to put on the Helmet of Salvation so I can be sure of who my identity is in Christ, and the breastplate of righteousness in place to stand up for what's right for me and my family.

God, I ask that you would help me buckle tightly the Belt of Truth around my waist, dispelling all of Satan's lies with the truth of God's word. Help me also to put on the Shoes of Peace, choosing peace everywhere that I go and sharing the Gospel of peace with others.

Lord, I also ask that you would help me lift my Sword of the Spirit and defend what you have given me and take back what belongs to me. I also pray that I will hold my Shield of Faith, oiled with confidence, up high as I go throughout my day.

Help me to use each piece of the Armor as I need to and know that no weapon forged against me will prevail. In Jesus Name...

AMEN!

Notes

1. Moore, Beth. *Breaking Free; Updated Edition.* Nashville: Lifeway Press, 1999. Print.

2. Swope, Renee. *A Confident Heart: How to Stop Doubting Yourself & Live in the Security of God's Promises.* Grand Rapids: Revell, 2011. E-book.

3. "salvation." *Merriam-Webster.com.* Merriam-Webster, 2014.Web. 9 August 2014.

4. "forged." *Merriam-Webster.com.* Merriam-Webster, 2014.Web. 9 August 2013.

About the Author

Michelle Moore is a wife and mother to two boys and lives near Dallas, Texas. She enjoys leading worship and bible studies at her home church, First at Firewheel, in Garland, Texas.

She has a degree from Collin College and plans to pursue wherever God's will takes her.

For More Information

You can check out Michelle Moore's blog at
www.myhearts-song.com and subscribe by email

Or

Like "Arm Yourself" on Facebook

Or

Follow Michelle on Twitter @MichelleM_MHS